Anonymous

Half Hours in the Wide West

Over Mountains, Rivers, And Prairies

Anonymous

Half Hours in the Wide West
Over Mountains, Rivers, And Prairies

ISBN/EAN: 9783744724166

Printed in Europe, USA, Canada, Australia, Japan

Cover: Foto ©ninafisch / pixelio.de

More available books at **www.hansebooks.com**

THE HALF HOUR LIBRARY
OF TRAVEL, NATURE AND SCIENCE
FOR YOUNG READERS.

HALF HOURS IN THE WIDE WEST

Over Mountains, Rivers, and Prairies

WITH NUMEROUS ILLUSTRATIONS

LONDON
DALDY, ISBISTER, & CO.
56, LUDGATE HILL
1877

CONTENTS.

BY CANOE AMONG THE IROQUOIS AND OJIBWAYS.

CHAP.		PAGE
I.	TORONTO TO THE MALINE RIVER	3
II.	THE MALINE RIVER TO WINNIPEG	15

BY INDIAN CARAVANS WESTWARD.

FROM WINNIPEG TO FORT EDMONTON 33

WINTER IN CANADA.

WINTER IN CANADA 57

NEW YORK TO CHICAGO.

I.	NEW YORK: ITS RIVER AND RAIL	77
II.	CHICAGO	94

ACROSS THE PRAIRIE BY RAIL.

I.	ST. LOUIS TO SALINA	111
II.	SALINA TO COLORADO SPRINGS	124

CONTENTS.

IN NEBRASKA.

CHAP.		PAGE
I.	AMONG THE OTOES	139
II.	THE PRAIRIE ON FIRE	151

IN COLORADO.

I.	AT COLORADO SPRINGS	163
II.	ITS CELEBRATED SIGHTS	179
III.	OVER THE RATONS	193

A MERCHANT OF THE FAR WEST.

I.	ADVENTURES	205
II.	ADVENTURES (*continued*)	216

IN THE YO SEMITE VALLEY.

I.	FROM SAN FRANCISCO	231
II.	FROM THE VERNAL FALL	244

BY COACH OVER THE SIERRA NEVADAS.

FROM PLACERVILLE TO VIRGINIA CITY 255

SALT LAKE CITY.

THE CITY AND ITS PEOPLE 279

BY COACH THROUGH INDIAN RAIDS.

SALT LAKE TO ATCHISON 297

A RIDE IN MEXICO.

I.	AMONG ROBBERS AND REVOLUTIONS	319
II.	AMONG ROBBERS AND REVOLUTIONS	329

LIST OF ILLUSTRATIONS.

	PAGE
THE BUFFALO HUNT	*Frontispiece.*
SHORES OF LAKE SUPERIOR	5
IROQUOIS WARRIOR	8
IROQUOIS WOMAN AND CHILD	9
BETWEEN LAKES	11
TRACES OF FOREST FIRE	13
ON THE MALINE; SHOOTING A RAPID	17
OAK POINT	19
FORT GARRY	21
OUR CAMP	22
INDIANS SPEARING SALMON	23
JUNCTION OF ASSINEBOINE AND RED RIVER	26
CAPTURING THE WILD HORSE	35
BLACKFEET HORSEMEN	39
CREE SQUAW WITH PAPOOSE	40
BUFFALO-SKIN LODGE, ON THE PRAIRIE	41
FALLS ON RAINY RIVER, CANOE AND LODGE . . .	43
AFTER THE BUFFALO	46
MAP OF MANITOBA	49
WINTER IN MANITOBA	53

	PAGE
STREET OF A CANADIAN CITY IN WINTER	59
DRIVING ON THE RIVERS	62
SUNSET ON THE ICE	64
WINTER FISHING	65
SKATERS AND ICE-YACHT	68
ENGINE AND SNOW-PLOUGH	70
WINTER IN THE BACK WOODS	73
THE BROADWAY, NEW YORK	79
VIEW IN CENTRAL PARK, NEW YORK	80
ON THE HUDSON	82
BRIDGE OVER THE NIAGARA	85
PULLMAN'S CARR, PACIFIC EXPRESS	89
TRAIN-TRANSPORT STEAMER	91
TRADERS' QUARTERS, CHICAGO, FORTY YEARS AGO	96
TRADERS' QUARTERS, CHICAGO, TO-DAY	97
A HALF-BREED	98
THE PRAIRIE TRAIN	113
DR. MILLER'S OFFICE	115
PRAIRIE RANCHE	119
PRAIRIE DOGS	121
CATTLE AND HORSES OF THE PRAIRIE	126
PRAIRIE HORSES AND CATTLE	127
THE BUFFALO	129
A RAILWAY PASS IN THE MOUNTAINS	132
MAIN STREET OF DENVER	133
AMONG THE ROCKY MOUNTAINS	135
VILLAGE OF THE DACOTAH INDIANS	141
FOREST CLEARING AND WATER SAW-MILL	143
A MOUNTED DACOTAH CHIEF	145
HORSES AND THE FIRE	154
THE REFUGE IN THE PRAIRIE FIRE	157
OUR SHANTY	164
THE UTE PASS	172
A COLORADO CANON	175

LIST OF ILLUSTRATIONS.

	PAGE
Gate of the Garden of the Gods	180
A Colorado Bridge	182
Hunting the Antelope	185
Monument Park	187
Monument Rocks	189
Ute Indians	191
Over the Ratons	195
Fisher's Peak	197
The Road at the Summit	199
A Caravan in California	211
Indian Attack upon a Merchant's Camp	218
Indian Man and Woman Mounted	221
Leaving the Pier at San Francisco	233
Interior of Cave	238
Entrance to the Cave	239
On the Hill-top	242
The Vernal Waterfall	245
A Roadside Stream	249
Mountain Scenery	257
Rain-bearing Clouds in the Sierra	261
A Small Geyser	263
Mount Davidson	265
Succession of Mountain Ranges	267
Hut on the Sierra	271
A Level Mountain Pass	274
Banks of Utah Lake	280
Banks of Utah Lake	281
A Street in Salt Lake City	283
Salt Lake at Sunset	292
Rocks in Echo Canon	298
A Mormon Caravan	300
A Mormon Caravan	301
On the Look-out	305
Mandan Indians	307

LIST OF ILLUSTRATIONS.

	PAGE
An Indian Raid on the Mail	311
A Mexican Hut	321
Mexican Vegetation	323
Sugar Canes	325
Road in a Barranca	327
A Pedrigal	332
A Pedrigal	333
Pronunciados attacking a Traveller	334
In the Zapotlan Market	335
Mirage on the Alkali Plains	339
Attack on Traveller by Robbers	343
Night among the Pineries	344

BY CANOE AMONG THE IROQUOIS
AND OJIBWAYS.

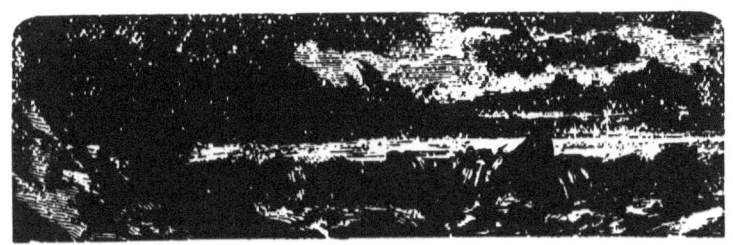

BY CANOE AMONG THE IROQUOIS AND OJIBWAYS.

CHAPTER I.

TORONTO TO THE MALINE RIVER.

OUR party of six started from Toronto. The first step in our journey was to get to Fort Garry, in the province of Manitoba.

That step is for giants, being at least a thousand miles long; the first half usually taken by a steamer along the Georgian Bay and the northern coasts of Lake Superior, the second half chiefly by canoes paddled or tugged over one of those innumerable chains of lakes that cover like network the vast rugged regions between the great basins of the St. Lawrence and of Hudson's Bay. A railway is proposed across this country from the Upper Ottawa to the Red River, which will open up incredible lumbering and mineral wealth, but in the meantime, to all travellers in search of something out of the way in locomotion, scenery, or living, we can cordially recommend our route.

The first five hundred and thirty miles of the route are by steamer, and as easy and as pleasant as a sail from one end of Loch Lomond to the other.

But why our inland seas should be called lakes, when the Baltic, Black, Caspian, Azov, Aral are called seas, is perhaps what no fellow can understand. That the former are reservoirs of fresh and those latter of salt water is the only reason assigned. But if saltness and not size entitles water to the name of sea, we have in the north-west a thousand saline lakes, each of which may lay claim to the title.

Of all the great lakes, Superior corresponds least to the ordinary conception of a lake. Day after day you can sail in the same direction over its deep crystal waters without seeing land. It breeds rains, storms, and fogs like the sea. It is cold in an American midsummer as the Atlantic. We heard from sailors stories of its strength and fury; but with the exception of a thunder-squall with which it greeted us as we entered between its portals, Capes Gros and Iroquois, our sail along its shores was as delightful as warm suns, bracing air, and cool nights could make it.

Superior has splendid harbours along its north coast. The two favourites are Nepigon Bay and Thunder Bay.

The scenery of Nepigon is the grandest in Ontario. Bluffs from three hundred to one thousand feet high rise from the water; some of them bare from sea to summit, others clad with graceful balsams or dark fir, the thick wood seamed with land-slides looking like steep highways through the forest.

Thunder Bay is farther west than Nepigon. It has sprung into note lately as the centre of extensive mining and prospecting.

SHORES OF LAKE SUPERIOR.

On the way, we pass Silver Islet, an insignificant-looking rock in a bay filled with islets similar in appearance. A wonderful vein of silver—probably the richest in the world—has been struck here, resembling in shape the trunk of a tree, which soon forks into two smaller trunks or branches. We were told that, in 1871, thirty men took out from the hole 1,200,000 dollars. More men could not get at it then, but authorities say that the probable value of the mine should be estimated in tens or hundreds of millions.

Valuable leads have been discovered in various places on or near the shores of the lake; and gold, copper, galena, and other minerals, have also been found and are being worked, without the same prodigious development of wild-cat mines which followed the discovery of the Ophir, and the Gould and Curry leads in Nevada.

Thunder Bay is a fine open harbour, with basaltic rock and island scenery second only to Nepigon. In 1870, when Colonel Wolseley's force disembarked at a spot called Prince Arthur's Landing, there were only two or three wooden shanties, but now there are one or two hundred, with some good buildings scattered along the shore.

The persistent loyalty of Canadians comes to the surface in the names they give to almost every new settlement. The number of Victorias, Prince Alberts, and other royal-family names already in the north-west promises a good crop of confusions and annoyances in postal matters in the future.

At Prince Arthur's Landing, Thunder Bay, we left the steamer, and commenced the second part of our journey to Fort Garry by "the Dawson Road." The incurable defect of this road for business purposes, or emigrants with much luggage, is that it consists of too many pieces.

The greater part of the distance is a wilderness of lakes and lakelets, separated from each other by spits, or ridges of granitic or gneissic rock. The Dawson Road across this may be described as consisting of three parts of unequal length; forty-five miles of land at the beginning, and one hundred and ten at the end, and three hundred and eighty miles, chiefly of water, between.

The first part of forty-five miles is from Thunder Bay to Shebandowán Lake. This we drove in one day in waggons light and heavy.

The second part of the Dawson Road—the lacustrine —will never be forgotten by us for its many novel pleasures. Only those who have enjoyed for successive days the motion of gondolas gliding over the water-streets of Venice, can understand the delights of canoeing.

Our canoes were four or five fathoms long, and, though fragile looking, each carried nine or ten men—six of them crew—and three or four hundred pounds' weight of luggage.

Our crews were chiefly Iroquois Indians from Caugh-naw-âga, near Montreal, the best voyageurs known, according to the testimony of every one who has tried them. The Iroquois made the engagement for the trip, and hired a few Ojibways between Shebandowán and Fort Francis to make up the necessary number. They were as fine-looking, clean-limbed men as one's eye could desire to rest on, punctual, diligent, uncomplaining, and reserving their chief affection for their canoes. As a jockey cherishes his horse and a shepherd his dog, so do they care for their canoe.

At every halting-place they turn it gently upside down, and carefully examine it and heal its wounds. The

IROQUOIS WARRIOR.

seams and crevices in the birch-bark yield at any extra strain, and scratches are constantly made by sunken brushwood in narrow channels or in shallow parts of the lakes. All such cracks or rents are daubed over with resin obtained from the red pine, which they always carry with them in an iron pot, till the bottom of an old canoe becomes actually covered with a black resinous

IROQUOIS WOMAN AND CHILD.

coat. The more uniform the blackness, the harder the service the canoe has seen.

On the larger lakes the Government has placed little steam-tugs, that towed our line of canoes and two large barges with immigrants. On the smaller lakes the Indians used their paddles, making from four to six miles an hour.

Dearly though they love fire-water, they do not carry it with them, and do not expect it from their employers; but a plug of tobacco enlivens them, and brings out snatches of song that break the monotony of the journey.

The two chiefs of the canoe are the captain, stationed at the bow, and the steersman, at the helm. Ignace Mentour, who had been with Sir George Simpson in many of his marvellously rapid and extended expeditions over the north-west, was the captain of our largest canoe; and Louis, who had been Sir George's cook at one time, was steersman. An English gentleman's household would be well ordered that had Ignace for coachman and Louis for butler. Many a day when we were on the prairies did we miss Louis's nice, clean cooking, and his tidy arrangement of kitchen stuff.

We became great friends with all our Iroquois, and could easily understand how it is that an Englishman travelling for weeks together with an Indian guide, invariably contracts a personal feeling amounting to friendship for him. His patience, endurance, and dignity, his fertility of resource and self-forgetfulness, are alike admirable, and can hardly fail to evoke friendship.

When the end of a lake was reached, work as heavy as paddling awaited the Indians. A portage of wooded rock, from fifty yards to two or three miles in length, had to be crossed to get to the next lake in the chain.

Their activity and rapidity of movement at these

BETWEEN LAKES.

portages were amazing. They worked as if a storm were coming on or an enemy chasing them.

The canoe was drawn up at the landing-place, emptied in a trice, turned up, examined, and if necessary caulked. Two of them would then shoulder it, and set off at a steady trot to the next lake. The others would hoist on their backs as heavy a load as a Constantinople porter is said to carry, and holding it together and in position by a strap passed across their foreheads, set off at a similar trot to the other end of the portage, throw down the load there, and run back for another, without a minute's halt; and so on, till all the luggage was portaged, and everything in readiness for starting on the next lake. The portage strap is broad in the middle, where adjusted to the forehead, and its great advantage to the voyager is that it leaves him the free use of his arms in going through the woods.

The shores of some of the lakes we canoed over had been desolated by fires, and much of their beauty marred. Others are as lovely as lakes can be that have no mountains rising from their shores.

The third lake in our chain, "Lac des Milles Lacs," and the last, called "Lake of the Woods," or wooded islands, are the most beautiful, and consequently many an Indian tale and tradition is connected with them. To be towed or paddled along those, with the sun shining on innumerable bays, creeks, channels, headlands, and islets of every form, is the perfection of pic-nic or holiday-making. We threaded our way through a maze of wood and water, where we would have pardoned a guide for making mistakes; but we went as surely as if on the king's highway, for an Indian on his own ground is never mistaken.

The islets are simply larger or smaller rocks of granite or gneiss, covered with a sprinkling of earth and a coat of moss, and wooded to the water's brink. The timber in most places is good, though not of the largest kind;

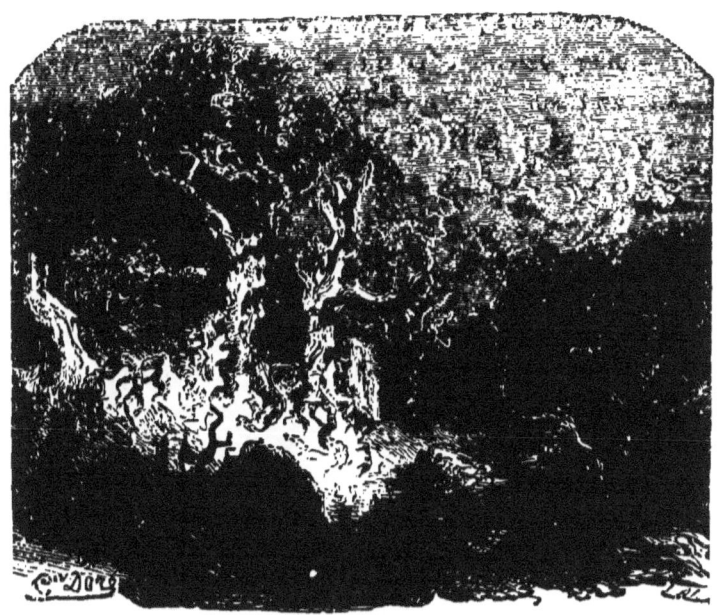

TRACES OF FOREST FIRE.

though how it happens to be so large, when the soil is so scant, is somewhat of a puzzle. Pine, aspen, and birch are the prevailing varieties. This abundance of wood is important, in view of its comparative scarcity on the great plains farther west.

At and near "the height of land," the streams connecting the lakes are very small, but as we go west they increase in size. The longest and most important is Rainy River, connecting Rainy Lake and Lake of the Woods. It is the boundary line between Canada and the United States for its ninety miles of length. The soil along its banks is exceedingly fertile, and I saw no more desirable place anywhere for a large settlement. Everything essential is in abundance; good wood, water, and soil; easy communication with the world east and west; and the Indian title now extinguished. There is not a single settler yet on the river, as far as I know.

On the Maline River, a short but broad and rapid stream, there are six or seven rapids, which must be shot or portaged round. We preferred shooting whenever it was practicable for our large and deeply-laden canoes.

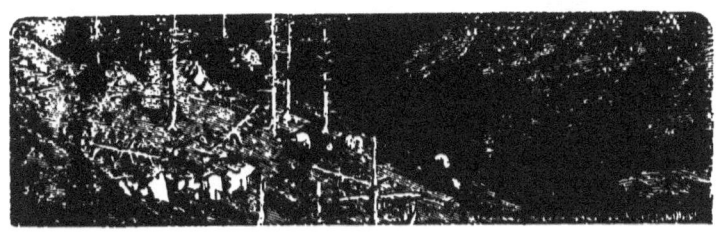

BY CANOE AMONG THE IROQUOIS AND OJIBWAYS.

CHAPTER II.

THE MALINE RIVER TO WINNIPEG.

TO shoot rapids in a canoe is a pleasure that comparatively few Englishmen have ever enjoyed, and no picture can give an idea of what it is. There is a fascination in the motion as of poetry or music. It must be experienced to be understood.

The excitement is greater than when on board a steamer, because you are so much nearer the boiling water, and the canoe seems such a fragile thing to contend with the mad forces, into the very thick of which it has to be steered.

Where the stream begins to descend, the water is an inclined plane, smooth and shining as glare ice. Beyond that it breaks into curling, gleaming rolls, which end off in white seething caldrons, where the water has broken on the rocks underneath. On the brink of the inclined plane the motion is so quiet that you think the canoe pauses for an instant. The captain is at the bow, a broader, stronger paddle than usual in his hand, eye kindling with enthusiasm, hand sure, and every nerve and fibre of his body at their utmost tension. The steersman is at his post, and every man is ready, knowing that a false stroke, or too weak a turn of their captain's wrist at the critical moment, means death.

A push with the paddles, and, straight and swift as an arrow, the canoe shoots down right into the mad vortex, now into a cross current that will twist her broadside round; but every man fights against it, and she steers right on to a rock, up to which she is being resistlessly sucked, and against which she will be dashed to pieces, but a rapid turn of the captain's paddle at the fit moment, and she rushes past, riding gallantly as a racehorse. The waves boil up at the sides threatening to engulf her; but nothing except a little spray or the cap of a wave gets in. On she speeds into the calm reach beyond, and all draw long breaths, and hope that another rapid is near.

The third part of the Dawson Road consists of one hundred and ten miles of low-lying, level land, from the north-west angle of the Lake of the Woods, to Fort Garry. Eighty miles of this are through woods growing either on marshes of rich deep black loam, or on light sandy and gravelly ridges and level tracts. Then we enter the

ON THE MALINE; SHOOTING A RAPID.

province of Manitoba, the western boundary of which is the eastern verge of the prairies, extending thence west to the Rocky Mountains.

None of us are likely to forget our first view of the prairies. It is almost as great an event in a lifetime as the first sight of the ocean.

OAK POINT.

We had arrived late at night, or rather at two o'clock in the morning, at Oak Point, the first post on the prairie, two miles in from the woods.

Wet to the skin, maddened by black flies, overpowered by fatigue and sleepiness, we came on the only building that was to be seen, a half-finished store of the Hudson's Bay Company. Untackling the horses, and letting them wander at their will to feed on the rich prairie grass, we entered an open door, barricaded unpleasantly with paint-pots, boxes, chips, and all sorts of things, and climbing up a rickety ladder to the second story, threw ourselves down on the floor, and slept heavily beside a crowd of teamsters whom no amount of shaking and kicking had been enough to awake.

The first noise in the morning that roused us was the joyful cry of the botanist of our party. "Thirty-two new species already! it's a perfect floral garden." We jumped up to see him with face all a-glow and arms full of treasures, and then looked out. A boundless sea of green, sprinkled with white, yellow, lilac, and red, extended all around. In the hollows the grass was from three to four feet high; on the level prairie from six inches to a foot.

The orders best represented in the flora were the Leguminosæ, Campanulaceæ, Rosaceæ, and Compositæ, the last especially, which is everywhere the characteristic order of the American flora. Asters and solidagos of all kinds were in greatest profusion. Tall, bright-yellow French marigolds and golden-rods in frequent clumps over the vast expanse gave a brilliant golden hue to the scene; and wild roses of all colours, blue and hare bells, and other plants then unknown to us, thickly bedded among the green grass, made up the most bright and beautiful carpet our eyes had ever looked upon.

We had reached the eastern boundary of Manitoba, the latest-born of the sisterhood now included in the dominion of Canada, and our first glance at her rich soil was reassuring. The Great West was a reality.

A drive of thirty miles over the prairie brought us to the Red River, a broad, deep, muddy-coloured stream, winding sluggishly through a land flat and level as Holland, till it empties itself into the great Lake Winnipeg to the north. Crossing the river in a scow, we drove through the village of Winnipeg to Fort Garry.

FORT GARRY.

The journey from Toronto to Fort Garry had taken us a fortnight; four days in the steamer, and ten in waggons and canoes.

The days, with one or two exceptions, were cool, bright, and sunny; the perfection of weather for travelling, in which existence was felt to be a blessing.

At nights we pitched tents on soft, open slopes, surrounded by thickwood, or on picturesque islets. After a long swim, and supper on hot, frizzling ham, that smelled wondrously savoury, and newly-made bread, washed down with incredible libations of tea, we threw ourselves on a floor of fragrant spruce boughs or rushes, to sleep the sleep of the just. One of the voyagers generally kept the fire burning all night, but his movements were so quiet that no one was ever disturbed.

OUR CAMP.

In the grey dawn, or a little before it, a cry of "Lève, lève" from the watchman brought us all to our feet. A look outside, first at the fire, which seemed to be smouldering at the stage at which it had been left six or seven hours before, a glance at the eastern sky, a hasty toilet, a hearty first breakfast, and we were once more in our canoes, gliding quietly down the mist-covered river, or over the shining waters of the lake.

The woods and waters were silent; a few flocks of wild pigeons or ducks, and an occasional small band of

INDIANS SPEARING SALMON.

Ojibway Indians, the only living creatures we came across tenanting those vast spaces.

The Ojibways of those lakes and woods between Lake Superior and Manitoba are pagans, with very distinct conceptions of the great Manitou, and a spirit-land beyond the setting sun. They are dirty in person and habits, unclean livers, cowardly, and even as compared with their brethren to the east, west, or south, low in the scale of civilisation.

Many of the lakes teem with fish, and as there is little soil to cultivate, except near Lake Superior, Rainy River, and a few other favoured spots, and little game in the woods, fish is their staff of life. Not that they would of themselves take to the cultivation of the soil, no matter how fertile and easily worked it might be. The Indian has never settled down to agricultural life, except under outside, that is, missionary influence. He is a nomad by nature, and the old nature crops out after years, I might say generations, of foreign teaching and customs alien to those of his forefathers.

And these Ojibways in particular are hard to reach. They are never together in large bodies, except for a few days at some religious ceremonial or grand *pow-wow*, when food has to be provided for them, and when the amount they eat is determined simply by the amount provided. The amount they can eat is, I believe, still an unknown quantity. Government has never had resources at hand sufficient to test their capacity. At all other times, each family or group is left pretty much to itself.

The tribal relationships are vague and ill-defined, and the authority of the chiefs nominal, when not sustained by popular personal gifts.

Usually a few families settle together on the banks of

a lake or river where pickerel and white-fish are abundant, live there till their camp gets too dirty, even for them, and then move off in their canoes to fresh woods and pastures new—and clean.

No pent-up Utica confines them; they are free to roam wherever they can canoe; for what the big canvas-covered bullock-waggon is to the emigrant on the plains, his canoe always is to the Ojibway. In it he carries wife and child, dog and musket, fishing-gear and pot. With these household gods he is independent of the great world. When on the march he lives in his canoe by day, he sleeps under it when it rains by night, and he carries it on his shoulders from lake to lake, as the snail carries his house on his back wherever he goes.

Valueless, agriculturally, as the land is, compared with the rich prairies to the west, the Ojibways are tenacious of their rights to it; and greater difficulty has been experienced in getting their consent to the extinguishing of their title than was experienced in dealing with their tribesmen or the Swampy Crees in Manitoba.

Theoretically, of course, their land belongs to the Queen; the title is vested in the Crown; but practically it belongs to the Indians, and, what is of most consequence, the Indians everywhere believe in their own rights. Their fathers lived, fought, wandered, and died on it; and though it takes at the rate of forty or fifty square miles to maintain a family according to their ancient style of living, there are estates as large, which nobody proposes to take from the owners, in Britain, where too the quantity of land is by no means so unlimited. The cheapest as well as the most honest way is to purchase their rights, to have the bargain confirmed

JUNCTION OF ASSINEBOINE AND RED RIVER.

by solemn treaty and all the etiquette they love so well, and then see that it is faithfully kept by our agents.

A little fair play, and a good deal of politeness, would have averted very many of those Indian wars that the history of America is so full of from the time of the Pilgrim Fathers to the Modoc war.

Low in the scale as these Ojibways are, they belong to a noble race. They speak a flexible, sonorous, musical language, and are generally well-developed physically. They are more given to oratory than other Indian tribes, and their chiefs seem to be partially selected for their oratorical powers. Has not their fish diet something to do with their inferiority of character to the Indians who live on buffalo-meat?

When they cannot get fish they starve, or, in a few cases, turn cannibals; but a *windego*, or cannibal, is said to be shunned by his fellows for ever after.

On the 30th of July, we reached Fort Garry, built on an angle formed by the junction of the Assineboine with the Red River.

That my readers may not be taken in at any time, now or hereafter, by the high-sounding title of "fort," it is only fair to say that a Hudson's Bay Fort is a square of wooden houses or shanties—the houses of the agent and servants, the store, blacksmith's shop in some cases, &c., surrounded by a paling or stockades fifteen to five-and-twenty feet high; and sometimes with small bastions at the angles to afford flanking defence. As the head-quarters of the Hudson's Bay Company, the depôt for pemmican and furs, it was surrounded with walls of masonry, and at the more exposed angles, circular towers, while over the gateway two six-pounders were mounted, looking in the direction of the little village of Winnipeg, that had struggled into existence half a mile out in the prairie to the rear of the fort.

Winnipeg did not present the most inviting appearance. Houses small, irregular, and frail enough in themselves, but looking doubly mean and contemptible compared with the wide level prairie on which they seemed to have dropped promiscuously, and which they disfigured horribly, straggled together into something like rows and streets; knots of loafers about the doors or bars—the latter chiefly—of numerous "saloons;" a semi-drunken Indian, dirty tattered blanket hanging loose about him, running excitedly from the village chased by imaginary foes;—such was our first picture or impression of the capital of Manitoba.

But to immigrants who knew a little about how Illinois, Iowa, and Minnesota had grown to their present population and wealth, there was nothing discouraging in these unhandsome first appearances.

The farmer from Ontario or the South, who had just arrived after a long, tedious march with his cattle and household goods, and pitched his tent outside the village, knew what he had come for. He looked at the soil, rich black loam everywhere, saw that the very streets might be turned into garden plots, knew that he had only to go into the Government office hard by to get a hundred and sixty acres for the asking, noticed that the children looked healthy, and straightway he took heart of grace, and felt that his coming was no mistake. He was not going to spend his time and money in Winnipeg.

To-morrow or next day he would hitch up and move off to his quarter-section. And in ten or twenty years, Winnipeg, just through the labours of such men on their farms, will be a very different place from the ragged, unbeautiful village of shanties and saloons of 1872.

BY INDIAN CARAVANS WESTWARD.

BY INDIAN CARAVANS WESTWARD.

FROM WINNIPEG TO FORT EDMONTON.

WHAT the birch-bark canoe is amid the network of lakes to the north and north-west of Huron and Superior, the horse is on the plains.

All that Crees, Blackfeet, or half-breeds really require here below are horses. Once on horseback, they can hunt buffalo with bows and arrows, if they possess not rifles; and having buffalo, they have all things.

After the hunt, they feast royally on the fresh meat; drying thin flitches of the most delicate parts in the hot sun, or hastily over the fire, they secure for immediate after-needs a supply of dried meat; pulverising all the rest, and mixing it with the melted fat in a bag made out of the hide, they have their much-loved pemmican, or pounded meat, an excellent condensed food for winter use. From the buffalo-hide they make their tents, their clothes, their moccasins, thongs, harness, and indeed everything they need.

It is no wonder that their explanation of the reason why the white man with his guns, powder, blankets, rum, and innumerable treasures is pouring into their country, is that there are no buffaloes in the white man's country, and that as life is not possible without the buffalo, he cannot help himself.

But the horse is even more important than the buffalo; for without the horse the buffalo is unattainable. Wild horses are found in nearly all the grassy plains of both North and South America, but their capture is no easy thing, and requires great skill, strength, and daring. The wealth of a tribe is estimated by the number of its horses, and almost all Indian wars begin with horse-stealing.

Horses, then, had to be provided to carry us westward across the prairies and through the mountains to British Columbia.

We contracted with a French half-breed called Emilien to supply the needed cavalcade for the first five hundred and thirty miles, or as far as Fort Carlton, on the Saskatchewan; and for the rest of the distance depended on being able to hire guides and horses at the Hudson Bay Company's posts along the route, and on a few Government horses which had been used the previous summer by surveyors, and left to winter at Forts Ellice and Edmonton.

Our party numbered six, but no less than thirty horses

CAPTURING THE WILD HORSE.

were required—six for ourselves, six for Emilien and his five men, eight for six baggage-carts and two buck-boards, and ten driven along in a pack—relays to relieve the saddle or cart horses occasionally, and enable us to travel at a speedier rate than would have been possible otherwise. Three of the men drove the six carts, two drove the pack of horses, and the sixth—an Irishman rejoicing in the name of Terence—undertook to act as cook, probably to learn the business.

The buck-boards were light springy vehicles, consisting of little else than four wheels and a seat, and intended to accommodate those for whom constant saddle exercise at the rate of forty or fifty miles a day might prove to be too much of a good thing.

Those two buck-boards did good service. They bowled along for nine hundred miles over the prairie trail, with its uneven surface and often deep ruts, through marshes and across rivers, up and down precipitous ascents, and yet when we came to the border of the woods near Edmonton, and had to abandon wheels, they seemed as good as new.

The Red River cart is also a wonderful piece of mechanism. The body is small, but the wheels are about seven feet in diameter, so that it looks all wheels and no body. It is made entirely of wood, and a few shaganappi, or buffalo raw-hide thongs. A cart without an ounce of iron was certainly a curiosity to us, but we soon found that it was the right thing in the right place. Ordinary carts would stick hopelessly in the mud at the crossings of the "creeks" and marshes, and travel slowly at other times; but the light high-wheeled Red River carts are borne up by the grass roots in the marshes, and on the ordinary trail the horses jog along with them at a slow, steady trot of four or five miles an hour.

If the axle, or any other part broke, the men were never at a loss. They would haul out a stick of white birch stowed near the tool-chest, shape it into something like the right thing, stick it in, tie it with shaganappi, and be jogging on at the old rate before a professional carriage-builder had made up his mind what was best to be done.

Some may wonder at the number of our carts. It is true that we got along with fewer after leaving Fort Carlton, but Emilien was a prudent man, and provided not only what was, but what might have been needed. He carried provisions for the whole party as far as Carlton, and for the return journey of his men, for he knew that we would not delay, nor even depart from the regular trail to hunt, and that as the noise of our company would be heard by large game more than a mile off, he could expect little for the pot on the way except a few prairie hens and wild duck.

The caravan is not more needed on the sandy deserts of the Old, than on the fertile but uninhabited prairies of the New, World. And at the rate at which we wished to travel, only two or three hundredweight of baggage could be put in each cart.

Soon after leaving Fort Garry, the addition of three

gentlemen and their servants to our party swelled the line of carts and horses to a length quite imposing in our ignorant eyes, but small compared to the long "brigades"

BLACKFEET HORSEMEN.

which go out twice a year from Red River, and half-breed settlements elsewhere, to hunt the buffalo on the

Qu'Appelle and the vast, almost waterless plains to the south and west.

From five hundred to a thousand half-breeds—men, women, and children—start together, with hundreds of horses and carts, oxen and dogs, and remain together out in the plains for two months at a time. The discipline

CREE SQUAW WITH PAPOOSE.

maintained by the half-breeds on these occasions is enough to prove what formidable enemies they could be if they were determined to prevent the settling of the country. They are all supplied with arms, they shoot and ride well, and could find food and water where regular troops would starve. They elect their own captains and policemen when out on the plains, set outposts, make camping laws and laws for the hunt, and strictly enforce them by fines, or the destruction of the clothes and gear of the offender, or by expulsion from the band.

BUFFALO-SKIN LODGE, ON THE PRAIRIE.

When near a great herd of buffalo, the excitement becomes intense. The approach is made cautiously, but not till the captain gives the word is the charge made. Then like hounds slipped from the leash, in the hunters dash, their horses quivering with the excitement of the riders.* Each man selects his cow or bull, and unless his horse trips in a mole or badger hole and throws him, he is taken safely within a few yards of its flanks. Aim is seldom missed, and the hunter dashes off instantly after another, and so on till the herd is far away. The half-breed would not exchange the pleasure of one such "run" for a whole year's profitable farm-work.

After the hunt, the work of the women and children begins. They have to prepare the dried meat and pemmican, and dress the hides. And when the carts are well filled, the band returns home.

Twenty-five days after we set out, we reached Fort Edmonton, nine hundred miles to the west, or rather the north-west.

A description of any one day's travel would do for the whole three weeks, so uniform and little startling were our experiences.

The day was divided into three "spells"—a word, I may say, that does much service all over the western part of America, where there are no milestones. At first it amused us to hear gentlemen gravely describe a lengthy march as "a good spell," or the camping-ground as a good or bad "spelling-place," but before getting to the Pacific we too used the phrases as if to the manner born. The distance between one halt and another is "a spell," part of that distance is "a piece." Before starting, ask "how far to the next halt," and you are told that it is either "a long" or "a short spell." The answerer seldom con-

* See Frontispiece.

descends to greater minuteness. Ask the same question after travelling a few miles, and then you have to go either "a good" or "a little piece."

Usually our camp was astir before earliest dawn. In

FALLS ON RAINY RIVER, CANOE AND LODGE.

camp life, sleep is so sound that every one acts on the Duke of Wellington's principle, that "when you begin to turn yourself in bed, it is time to turn out." The first one or more that awaked kindled the fire, and if a look at the sky showed that it was too early to call the others, they would go off to see if the horses were grazing at hand and all right. If it was near sunrising, the loud cry of "Leve! lève!" brought every one to his feet.

Terry was infusing the tea for our morning cup the first time that he heard this cry, and turning round quickly, indignantly asked the astonished half-breed what he wanted to "lave" so soon for? He "wasn't going to lave till he had his tay."

Toilets were made in a hurry; when near river or lake, a dip was enjoyed by most of us; blankets were folded, tents struck and packed, the horses brought in, and by this time Terry had the tea ready. Even in July and August on our prairies, the nights and mornings are so cool that the hot fragrant tea is welcome. Each man gets about a quart ladled out into his pannikin, and that with a junk of bread or biscuit is the first meal. Everything is now stowed securely in the carts. Each man saddles his own horse, and before sunrise we are off.

Who that has enjoyed those morning gallops across the prairies can ever forget them?

The English highwayman of last century smacked his lips at the foot of the gallows when unadvisedly reminded by the chaplain of his sinful moonlight rides on Blackheath. But the greater sense of freedom and exhilaration of spirits on the prairies outweighs even the sweetness that comes from doing things forbidden.

Vast stretches of virgin land lay before and all around us; not a dull, unbroken, monotonous expanse, but at one time swelling uplands rose and fell for mile after mile, enclosing lakelets in their hollows, fringed with tall reeds, or lapped in soft willows; at another, long reaches of rich lowlands, extending to a far horizon like the sea, broken by islets of aspens that seemed to rise out of the levels like bold bluffs. To-day we would ride endlessly through avenues of whispering trees, so trim and beautiful that we imagined that soon the lodge or gate must be reached, and the house of the owner seen crowning one of the open hillsides that spread gently away far to the right and left. To-morrow the course was across a treeless plain, covered with short grass and without sign of wood or water, flat as your hand in one place, and in another a succession of saucer or cup-like depressions.

So we rode on, stage after stage, deeper into the heart of this great lone land, proud that it belonged to the English, and wondering that it should be unknown. The air was fresh and flower-scented, and the weather simply perfection for travellers. Each morning brought variety, but always a repetition of the keen sense of animal enjoyment.

To get a good gallop without touching the horses with whip or spur, all that we had to do at any time was to drop a mile or two behind the carts, and then give our beasts the rein. So eager are they to be with their companions, that the dullest of them then does his "level best." We never saw the gregariousness of the horse exhibited so strongly as on this journey; and on the Pacific slope the instinct amounts to ferocity when interfered with.

Occasionally the occupations of our journey were relieved by suddenly and unexpectedly coming up with a small herd of buffaloes, to which we gave chase. Then the fire and speed of our half-wild steeds rose to their highest. Though the chase always ended in the escape

AFTER THE BUFFALO.

of the buffaloes, it produced an amount of excitement and delight too keen to be ever forgotten.

As we rode on the trail, or through the long grass wet with dew, the prairie hen would run for a few yards near our feet, and then try a short low flight, like the Scotch grouse, or the wild pigeon or partridge take wing from the nearest tree, or a flock of ducks rise from the marsh or pool by the side of the road.

The rosy fingers spreading over the sky, succeeded by the paler light, always warned us to turn round and see the sun rise, as he rises out of the sea; and by comparing the exact minute with that of sunset, the local time and the longitude of the place we were in could be roughly determined.

A jog-trot by the side of the carts for an hour or two, or a walk to rest the horses, brought us to the first ".spelling place." Untackle and unharness the patient, willing brutes, drive them to the water, and then let them feed on the nutritious prairie grasses during the halt; hurry up the breakfast of bread, tea, fried pork, or pemmican, varied by the contributions of the gun, if there is time to cook them, and fall to with appetites greedy as the grave.

The second "spell" is like the first, except that the sun has warmed the air and dried the grass. The mosquitoes are a pest, but like mightier beings, not so bad as they have been painted. Dinner is a repetition of breakfast. Then follows the afternoon "spell," the length of it—as of the others, a few miles less or more—being determined by the distance that has to be travelled before reaching a good place to rest.

Our aim is to make between thirty-five and fifty miles in the course of the day, and our only anxiety is to have a good camping-ground for the night. Good feed for the horses and water are indispensable. Wood near at hand is desirable And if an elevated spot, free from mosquitoes and rich in flowers, can be had, so much the better. At supper we can afford to take our time, and extra cooking is therefore usually reserved for it—our fourth meal; and as the dew falls heavily, we eat it in the chief's tent. When fresh buffalo meat is to be had at any of the forts, a supply sufficient to last for three or four days is usually given to us, and everything else in the larder is then "of no account." Buffalo-steak is tender and juicy as any porter-house or rump-steak, and the fat is sweet and delicate as butter.

Sunday was the most pleasant day of the week. At first Emilien objected to resting, as he had always been accustomed to travel on every day alike; but before the long journey was over, he confessed that less speed would have been made on his than on our plan, not to speak of sundry other advantages of the periodical rests to men and horses.

On Saturday evening the best possible camping-ground was selected; and rather than pass a particularly good place, the halt was called in the afternoon. The botanist would then go off to ramble far and wide. Some would take their guns or fishing-lines. Others would do up their week's or fortnight's washing. Carts and buckboards were carefully looked to by the men, valises unpacked, and everything made ready for the enjoyment of a good long rest.

MAP OF MANITOBAH.

Especially on the prairies and in the mountains is the weekly rest a physical blessing.

All through the week there has been a rush and a strain. The camp begins to be astir at three A.M., and from that hour till nine or ten o'clock at night, constant high pressure is kept up. At the halting-places meals have to be cooked, horses looked to, baggage arranged and rearranged, harness, carts, or pack-saddles mended, clothes washed or dried, observations and notes taken, specimens collected, and everything kept clean and trim.

No rest is possible. Only from four to six hours of sleep can be snatched. The pure air, the novelty, and excitement sustain a tourist, so that on Saturday night he possibly grudges what seems the unnecessary loss of a day. But if he pushes on, he is apt to lose all the benefit to his health that he has gained, while men and horses get jaded and spiritless.

But the great advantages of the day to a party of travellers are lost when each man is left the whole time to look after himself, as if there was no common bond of union, and no sacredness about the day. They then sleep or gamble; ramble or shoot; snare prairie squirrels or prairie dogs; read, write, eat, and drink; are benefited as their horses are, but nothing more, perhaps less. There is a more excellent way, for the Sabbath was made for the whole man. Let the head of the party ask all to meet for common prayer, without asking, "What denomination are you of?" They will gladly come if they believe that they are welcome. The singing of a hymn is usually enough to bring them round the tent or hillock, where the service is held. The kneeling together, the alternate reading, and a few earnest, kindly words do more than anything else to stir the better nature, to awaken old blessed remembrances, to heal up the little bitternesses and squabbles of the week, and to produce that sympathy that makes each member of the party consider the interests of the whole.

They have been brought into the presence of God, and the rest of the day is hallowed by that hour. Cut off from the busy world, they are made to feel their dependence on each other; and master and man are all the better for it.

On Monday morning, the start was always made at an earlier hour than on other days, and longer marches travelled.

And now what about the country : this "fertile belt" that so much has been written about?

We found what we saw of it to be all that the most enthusiastic tourists had painted. True, we saw it in the summer, when it is bright and beautiful, with all the characteristic flowers of the American flora; when cool nights followed warm, sunny, cloudless days; when although wood was sometimes scarce, we could carry enough in our carts to cook the night's and morning's meals; and though often the lakelets were saline, enough fresh water could always be had from a spring or marsh.

That it is very different from December to April, I can well believe. Even where the country is well wooded, a

FROM WINNIPEG TO FORT EDMONTON. 53

North American winter scene has a look of desolation to one accustomed to milder climes; but the vast uninhabited prairie in winter must be terrible. One unbroken field of snow, relieved by no colour, no signs of life, no shelter from the drifts and the biting frost—who would make his home in such a land?

WINTER IN MANITOBA.

And yet not only Indians and half-breeds, but whites, sleep in the open air and enjoy their sleep, the thermometer I am afraid to say how many degrees below zero, and with the protection only of a blanket and a buffalo robe. The climate may not be adapted for Fantees or South-Sea Islanders; but it is for men of manly mould and manly strength, and those are the men—the men of Northern and Central Europe. I met new settlers in Manitoba from the eastern provinces of the Dominion, and their testimony was unanimous on the point that they suffered less from cold and from colds in their new than in their old homes. The snow is· dry as meal or sand from December to March. The children can run about in moccasins without getting their feet wet, and as no crust forms on the snow till the first thaws of spring, the horses, and even the cattle, can " dig " or paw it off, and feed on the grass underneath. The sky is bright and cloudless, the air bracing, and the long nights are illumined with an untroubled moon or a marvellous splendour of stars.

WINTER IN CANADA.

WINTER IN CANADA.

IT is with no feelings of dread that Canadians look forward to the winter's shroud that is to wrap up all nature in the stillness of death. On the contrary, they long for it.

They are, however, fastidious about the proper timing of the fall.

Great is the disappointment when it comes before the ground is sufficiently indurated by frost, or the lakes and rivers have acquired a sufficient crust of ice. In that case, the snow acts as a warm covering, the ice beneath ceases to increase in thickness, and a treacherous footing, during the whole winter, is the necessary consequence.

Great is the joy, on the other hand, when no snow falls till the ice is able to bear the skater or the sleigh, and the earth is hard as iron.

This kindly feeling towards the snow can be accounted for on various grounds.

The sudden sinking of the temperature, along with the fall of snow, produces a wonderful exhilaration of spirits. The languor induced by the extreme heat of summer is at once banished; and men and animals seem intoxicated with the new and bracing conditions of the atmosphere. The small Normandy horses prance with delight, and can hardly be reined in. The Newfoundland dogs roll in ecstasy in the snow. A Canadian feat, which at first looks like a traveller's story, viz., the lighting of gas by merely pointing the finger to the burner, is accounted for by the dryness of the atmosphere. The performer first shuffles with his feet along the carpet; and, in presenting his finger to the burner, a spark of electricity is emitted which is sufficient to produce the effect. The friction of the foot develops the electricity, which is conducted by the body to the point of emission. This feat, however, can be performed only in very low temperatures, and when the room is heated by a stove.

Sometimes the difference between the temperature of the room and that of the external atmosphere is 100°, so that the most favourable conditions are afforded for the development of electricity.

Another reason for welcoming the snow is the important consideration, that the country becomes a universal highway.

Nature macadamizes the whole country, and the settlers, shut up in the back woods, have now free access to the towns and cities. The lumberers can now drag their logs to the railway or the river, and fire-wood sinks in price

STREET OF A CANADIAN CITY IN WINTER.

as soon as the carriage becomes easy. Wheeled carriages disappear from the roads and streets; and the sleigh, which is the peculiarly national vehicle of the Canadians, takes their place.

The sleigh is seen in every variety of form; but it essentially consists of a shallow, oblong body set upon a pair of skates or runners. That of the farmer is of the rudest form, with buffalo skins upon the cross seats. The more affluent citizens decorate their sleighs with gay trappings and bear-skins, which flaunt over the back of the vehicle. The wheeled carriages are generally inelegant and inconvenient, but all the resources of the coach-builder are employed to render the sleigh both elegant and luxurious.

To a stranger, a drive in a sleigh is a new and delightful sensation. The rapid pace, the smooth and noiseless motion, the bright sunshine, the joyous excitement of the horses, the bracing atmosphere, all combine to refresh and exhilarate.

The Canadian goes out for a pleasure drive at a temperature far below zero, and that in his open vehicle, while in England nothing but dire necessity would warrant one to go abroad in similar circumstances. This does not arise from the superior hardiness of the Canadian, for he is much more sensitive to cold than the Englishman who has newly arrived in the country. It is due altogether to the peculiarities of the climate.

One never feels in Canada the raw, chilling cold which pierces through the whole frame in England. This is also ascribed to the dryness of the air, but it is more probably owing to the highly oxygenated state of the atmosphere —a given amount of inhalation assimilating a greater amount of oxygen, and thus producing a greater degree of animal heat.

The natives and old residents usually wear fur caps and

DRIVING ON THE RIVERS.

gloves, but the Englishman, when he first goes out, feels no necessity for any change in his apparel. In a few years, however, he is glad to adopt the customs of the country. At first, the temperature of the rooms is intolerable, but he gradually comes to acknowledge their comfort.

There is still a third reason for the glad welcome of winter, viz., that it is the great holiday season of Canada.

Agricultural labour ceases, the navigation is closed, and commerce is no longer active. The winter is devoted to social entertainments and outdoor amusements. In these amusements the snow and ice are turned to excellent account.

As soon as the margins of the lakes are frozen, the ice is thronged with skaters. This amusement is not confined to the male sex. The Canadian ladies are seen in equal numbers on the ice, and often excel the stronger sex in rapidity of movement and gracefulness of evolution. Great distances are often accomplished during a morning's exercise. A favourite feat is to circle round some of the group of the thousand islands at the lower end of Lake Ontario, and explore the winter aspects of this the most striking scenery of Canada.

One of the finest sights is to witness the setting of the sun upon the frozen lake while the skaters crowd the ice. The red glare of the sun communicates a peculiar hue to the ice, and as the group of skaters, with glancing steel, glide between you and the fiery ball, you feel that you have a truly Canadian scene presented to you.

In the sunsets of Canada there is a tint which is never seen in England. It is a deep apple green. It is seen in its greatest intensity only in the Lower St. Lawrence, and it is worth while taking this route from England, notwithstanding its hazardousness, were it only to enjoy the gorgeous sunsets in autumn.

It is not often that the Canadians can enjoy skating on their lakes and rivers. When the snow falls, the ice is spoiled for the rest of the winter, as the covering remains the whole season. When their amusement is suddenly

SUNSET ON THE ICE.

curtailed by a fall of snow they have resort to the device of artificial rinks.

An extensive piece of ground is levelled and covered in by a wooden shed. The area is flooded with water at night, and a smooth surface is formed by the morning.

A thin sheet of water is added every day to obliterate the roughening effect of the day's exercises. The rink is lighted up at night, so that the amusement may be continued after sunset.

WINTER FISHING.

Such a resource is very valuable in a country where the snow renders walking exercise very difficult. The children, instead of being cooped up in heated rooms, are sent to take a few hours' exercise in the skating rink, to which the family subscribes.

It is only in the shallower part of the great lakes that the water freezes. The depth of water is so great, that it is only at the margin a crust is formed. The St. Lawrence, however, is frozen through nearly its whole extent, so that, in the case of an invasion from the American side, the attacking force could readily advance on foot against all the great cities and fortresses of Canada. The rigour of winter, however, will always prove a formidable barrier to an advancing enemy.

Snow-shoeing is also a favourite amusement, though a stranger cannot well understand the source of the pleasure it affords.

To the Indian and the backwoodsman it is often useful, as without the broad support which the snow-shoe gives, it would be impossible to move across the country: but when snow-shoeing is resorted to as an amusement, it is more for the difficulty than the ease of walking it is employed. Instead of easily moving along the beaten track with ordinary shoes, a snow-shoe walker seeks the untrodden snow, that he may display his agility encumbered by serious clogs to his movements.

The movement is very ungainly, as the feet require to be so far apart, and this awkwardness is greatly increased when an attempt is made to run; and snow-shoe races are common during the winter.

Snow-shoeing forms a regular part of military drill. It is quite conceivable, that the use of snow-shoes, in certain military movements, would give one body of men a great advantage over another, and, in former military operations in Canada, the advantage has been tested.

Taboganing is an amusement borrowed from the Indians.

The tabogan consists simply of a light board, or the bark of a tree, shaped somewhat like a sleigh. It is brought to the top of a slope, the party sits upon it, and he immediately glides down with a rapidity proportioned to the steepness of the incline.

At Quebec, the cone of ice formed by the spray of the Montmorency Falls is employed for this purpose. Grave senators, as a relaxation from the duties of parliament, resort to the cone to enjoy this exciting and bracing exercise. The only disadvantage is, that at every trip the party must carry both the tabogan and himself to the summit of the cone; but the rapid descent seems to be an ample compensation.

The Scotch have brought with them to Canada the national game of curling, and it is enjoyed, like skating, under cover. The curling-stone, though retaining the name, is made of iron, as stone, in low temperatures, is found to be a material much too brittle. Though introduced by the Scotch, the game is a favourite one with all the nationalities.

The most remarkable device of the Canadian to gain amusement in his winter fetters is the ice-boat. It is startling in the extreme to see it glide with railway speed across the ice like a phantom ship.

At a distance, it appears precisely like a small yacht

with its sails set. It is simply a boat set upon a pair of long skates or runners. It is managed much like an ordinary boat, and, so smoothly does it glide, that in a side wind it actually goes faster than the wind itself.

SKATERS AND ICE-YACHT.

When there is only a light breeze blowing, one is surprised to see the boat shooting across the lake as if impelled by a stiff gale. She can sail nearer to the wind than if in water, and the bite of the skate prevents her making any lee-way.

This device is not turned to any practical account; the object aimed at is simply to enjoy the sensation of rapid locomotion, which, in all forms, seems to be very grateful to a Canadian's feelings.

A stranger, on first landing in Canada, is at once struck with the more rapid rate at which all vehicles move. Even waggons, heavily laden, are drawn by horses at a trotting pace. The leisurely walk of the cart-horse of the old country is unknown in Canada.

The only exception to the rule of rapid locomotion is the railway.

The Grand Trunk, which runs along the whole length of the St. Lawrence and Lake Ontario, is both slow and safe, and the safety is due to the slowness. Accidents frequently occur, but they are not very destructive to life or property. One train may run into another, or get off the track, but the injury is comparatively slight when the speed is only fifteen or twenty miles an hour.

When the speed is increased, the destructive power increases in a much higher ratio. When it is doubled, the destructive power is increased fourfold; or, in other words, the destructive power increases as the square of the velocity.

The danger on English railways arises from the demand of the people for speed.

In winter, the difficulty of railway travelling is so great that the sleigh frequently asserts its superiority. In Toronto and Montreal, the street railway system is adopted, but the snow drives the cars off, and large sleighs are employed instead, so that, for a considerable part of the year, the rails are practically useless.

The railway, unlike the sleigh, was not intended, in its original construction, to struggle against the rigour of an almost arctic climate.

ENGINE AND SNOW-PLOUGH.

In a snowdrift, the locomotive is like a maddened bull charging its enemy with the greatest impetuosity. It plunges into the snow, then backs out ; and, with deep-drawn breath, renews the charge ; but frequently its rage is impotent, it gives up the task in despair, and the slow process of the shovel must be resorted to.

Engines carry in front a snow-plough for clearing the rails, but this is effectual only when the drift is not formidable. Sometimes three or four engines come to the rescue of a train buried in the snow, and with their united strength, charge through the opposing drift.

It is not an uncommon incident of Canadian travel to be snowed up in a cutting on a railway. The snow of Canada almost invariably falls in the form of fine, white dust, consisting of separate gritty crystals. The large flakes of England are scarcely ever seen. This dry form of snow is much more liable to drift, and, with the slightest wind, it comes pouring over the edge of a cutting in the railway like sand pouring down from a sand-glass.

It is one of the most unpleasant things in travel, to be caught in one of these drifts. You may be in the midst of a forest, far from help; and the Canadian railways do not carry provisions, like those of their more provident neighbours in the United States. The firewood may fail while you are under the snow at a temperature below zero, and you may have the prospect of being snowed up for days in this miserable plight.

We had once the misfortune of being snowed up, along with many others, when we had an unexpected rescue from our impending fate. We stuck fast in the wreath, after the usual attempts to push through. We could not even back out, and retreat to some spot where there was less chance of being buried up.

When all the usual expedients were tried and failed, an American volunteered to go under the machinery, and shovel out the snow that clogged its movements. He worked on with a hearty good-will, but it was all in vain; besides, the feed-pipe was frozen, so that the boiler could not be supplied with water from the tender.

All the passengers had now given themselves up to blank despair. Night was fast coming on, and there was every prospect of spending it in the train, without food, and without the ordinary comfort of a sleeping car. The snow began gradually to rise around the carriages. It reached the windows, and then the light began to be gradually shut out by the ever-rising stratum. All looked wistfully through the narrowing chinks of the windows, and each had his speculations as to the dreary night coming on, and the thoughts of anxious friends at home.

The situation was, however, not so miserable as to prevent one from admiring the beautiful forms assumed by the snow as it rose around the carriages. Our snow studies were soon curtailed by the closing in of night, and the pangs of hunger began to assail the whole company, with no hope of having them appeased.

It was like an angel's visit when a boy, with a Scotch accent, stepped into the carriage with a pitcher of hot tea, and a basket full of bread and cheese. This was sent by his mother, and he was told not to take anything for it.

Many were the blessings on the good woman for her

timely supply. Her kindness, however, did not end here. She sent down her eldest son to the train with the instruction, that if he saw any "kent body," he should ask him to spend the night at her house.

We were fortunate in sharing the invitation; but it was with no little difficulty we reached the settlement in the

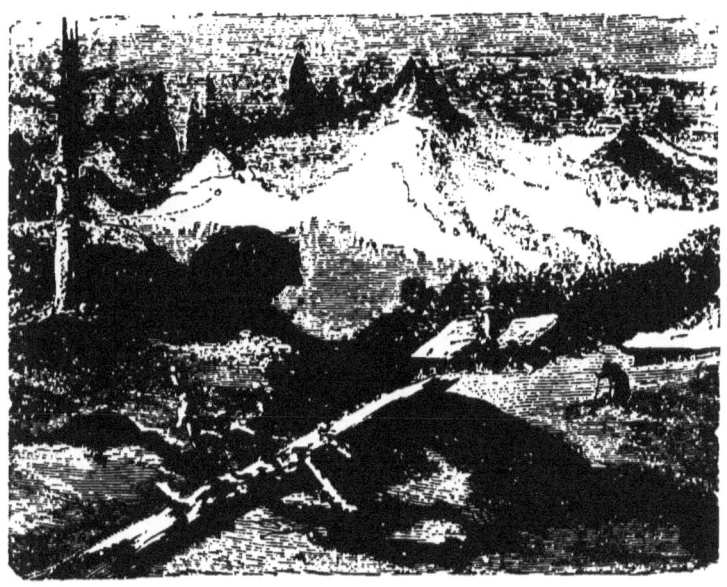

WINTER IN THE BACK WOODS.

cleared forest. The snow, thawed by the sun, and subsequently frozen, forms a treacherous crust, which now bears you up, but the next moment allows you to sink to unknown depths.

The deer is, from the same cause, easily killed in

winter, as its small foot sinks through the crust, while the broader foot of the hunter bears him up.

When we arrived at the farm-house, we were first ushered into the large kitchen, where we found the patriarch of the family sitting by the stove, with his daughter, son-in-law, and numerous grandchildren, all intent on showing hospitality to the rescued strangers.

There could not be a finer picture than this homestead, of the successful career of a Canadian settler. And it is the rule for the industrious settler to achieve similar success.

NEW YORK TO CHICAGO.

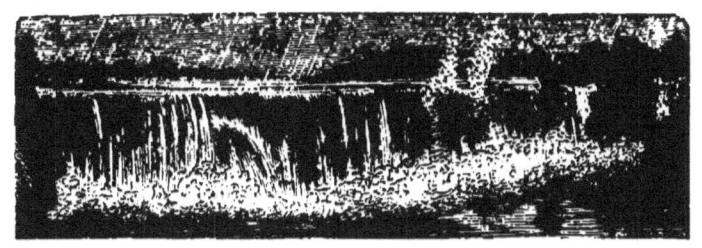

NEW YORK TO CHICAGO.

CHAPTER I.

NEW YORK: ITS RIVER AND RAIL.

WHEN I first saw New York it did not appear to me a foreign city in the same sense as Paris, or Frankfort, or Milan. A closer and more leisurely examination produced a different impression.

To walk along Broadway recalls a walk along Regent Street, but it also recalls a walk along the Rue de la Paix. What seems to be English is rivalled, if not outdone, by what is unmistakably French, while many things have neither a French nor an English impress.

The architectural effects are extraordinary in their variety. The want of simplicity and repose is as marked as the absence of a distinctively national style. Every one has apparently followed the bent of his fancy, and the straining after originality has led to a confusion of ideas and a clashing of aims.

All nationalities seem to have sent their representatives to this city. Half the languages of Europe are spoken by the motley gathering. The English tongue is in the ascendant; but the eye fails to see many figures or faces to match the hereditary language. The ladies are dressed after the latest French mode, yet the fashion of their apparel is the only thing they have borrowed from Paris. Their looks are native to the soil, and to call them good is not to speak of them in language sufficiently eulogistic. The men are dressed with a regard for appearances which is more common in Paris than in London. There is none of the uniformity in their attire which is akin to monotony. All do not seem to have been condemned, by a law which cannot be gainsayed, to wear the same hideous hat. The "wideawake" is as common as the "chimney-pot," and the mixture of the two produces a pleasing effect.

The purity of the air is delicious. If a dwelling be built of marble, or brick, or stone, the beholder has no difficulty in pronouncing as to the nature of the material, and has the satisfaction of duly appreciating the whiteness of the delicate marble, the warmth of the brick, the solidity of the stone.

The principal streets are broad; the principal squares are spacious. The several Avenues, which run parallel to each other throughout the greater part of the city, are so wide that the tramways which are laid in them do not in the slightest degree interfere with the traffic. For the passage of all conveyances there is room enough and to spare.

THE BROADWAY, NEW YORK.

At the upper end of the city is the Central Park. This public ground covers an area of more than eight hundred acres. It is laid out in a style resembling the Bois de Boulogne rather than Hyde Park and Kensington Gardens. Several years hence, when the trees shall have attained

VIEW IN CENTRAL PARK, NEW YORK.

their full height, the Central Park will be second to no other place of the kind.

Quite as remarkable as the cosmopolitan aspect of

New York streets is the contrast between the different portions of the city. The business quarter has a finished and substantial look; the offices seem as if they had been built for some time. Proceeding westward, the several edifices are evidently built for show, and are apparently of comparatively recent date. In the former case the buildings have a money-making impress upon them; in the latter the stamp of the successful millionaire is unmistakable.

From the fine mansions of the rich in a fashionable Avenue, the transition is rapid to the miserable shanty of the Irish squatter. At the one end gorgeous carriages roll along; at the other, geese are feeding among the grass. Another contrast is that between the splendour of the buildings and the wretchedness of the pavement. The streets are filled with ruts. For this the "City Fathers" are severely censured; but they can afford to brave the indignation of their fellow-citizens so long as they are permitted to hold office and to deal with the funds at their disposal in the manner most pleasing to themselves.

In my opinion scant justice has yet been done to New York on the whole. It has its drawbacks, as has every city on the face of the globe, but it possesses excellencies which more than outweigh them. The man of business finds it as good a centre for his operations as London. The pleasure-seeker can amuse himself as well as in Paris, while men of letters and students of art affirm that the prospects of New York becoming an honoured home of literature and art grow brighter every day.

82 NEW YORK TO CHICAGO.

To reach Chicago, should time be no object, we cannot

ON THE HUDSON.

do better than ascend the Hudson River in a steamboat.

to Albany, and enter the train there instead of at New York.

The scenery of the Hudson has been highly lauded, but not overpraised. It is quite as romantic as that of the Rhine. In the autumn the aspect of the woods on the river's banks and heights, clothed in the gorgeous tints of that season, is a spectacle of wonderful beauty. The vine-clad hills between Coblentz and Bingen, when seen at their best, cannot match the Hudson in its most picturesque parts. Nature has done much for that river. One thing, however, is wanting to render it as famous as its European rival; the Hudson has not yet had its Byron. While no great poet has rendered it attractive by his inspired verse, a steamboat company has endeavoured to create an interest of a more prosaic and more practical kind. The steamers which ply between New York and Albany are marvels in their way. To call them "floating palaces" is not the language of hyperbole, but is the simple truth.

Let me suppose that the traveller starts from New York in the evening by the Pacific Express. On the morning of the following day he arrives at Rochester, where "Pullman's Palace Cars" are attached to the train; he gets a good view of Niagara Falls as the train slowly crosses the bridge over the boiling rapids, sees a large portion of the Western section of Canada, and then, after having passed two nights and one day in a railway carriage and traversed a distance of nine hundred miles, he arrives at Chicago.

Hamilton is the first Canadian city of note at which a stoppage is made. Situated at the western extremity of Lake Ontario, and having communication by water and rail with the principal cities of Canada and with the capitals of the Eastern States of America, the city of Hamilton has many chances in its favour. It has prospered hitherto, notwithstanding the mistakes made by those of its citizens who, in their eagerness to advance, incurred an amount of indebtedness which they found it difficult to discharge to the perfect satisfaction of many English bond-holders. However, the days of rash speculation are said to have passed away, and the lessons learned have been profitable. At Hamilton station the passengers dine, with the exception of those who are so fortunate as to have secured seats in the Hotel Car attached to the train. The occupants of this car take their meals " on board.".

I had heard much said in praise of " Pullman's Palace Cars," but I was unprepared for the reality. The first trip in one of these cars forms an epoch in a traveller's life. To one accustomed to English railway carriages they are specially welcome. The contrast between the waggon in which Roderick Random journeyed to London and a modern carriage, is not much greater than the contrast between life on the rail in an English first-class carriage and in a Pullman's car. In order to form a fair notion of the character of the latter it is but necessary to recall the descriptions of those luxurious saloon carriages which the directors of our railways have had constructed

BRIDGE OVER THE NIAGARA.

for the use of the Queen. No Royal personage can be more comfortably housed than the occupant of a Pullman car, provided the car be an hotel one. In the train by which I travelled, one out of the three sleeping cars was of the latter description.

The Hotel Car is divided into sections, forming state rooms, wherein parties of four can be accommodated. Between these rooms are seats arranged in the usual way. At the rear is a kitchen, which, though small, contains every appliance necessary for cooking purposes. There are water tanks, in which is stored a supply of water for washing and drinking sufficient to last the journey. A wine cellar contains the liquors which are likely to be in demand, and an ice-house preserves ice for the gratification of those who prefer cold beverages.

At stated intervals the conductor walks round, taking the passengers' orders, who make their selections from the bill of fare. The choice is by no means small. Five different kinds of bread, four sorts of cold meat, six hot dishes, to say nothing of eggs cooked in seven different ways, and all the seasonable vegetables and fruits, form a variety from which the most dainty eater might easily find something to tickle his palate, and the ravenous to satisfy his appetite. The meal is served on a table temporarily fixed to the side of the car, and removed when no longer required.

To breakfast, dine, and sup in this style while the train is speeding along at the rate of nearly thirty miles an hour, is a sensation of which the novelty is not greater than the comfort. An additional zest is given to the good things by the thought that the passengers in the other cars must rush out when the refreshment station is reached, and hastily swallow an ill-cooked meal. It is proposed to construct dining cars which will be at the service of all who travel by the train; and when this is done, the limit to improvement will almost have been reached.

Yet it would be a mistake to assign any bounds to the possibilities connected with railway travel in the United States, and in the Western States in particular. No prejudices exist against novelties, nor are the directors of the several companies able to scorn the demands of the travelling public for increased comforts and conveniences.

So many railways run between the same points that competition forces each company to outbid its rivals. In other countries reduction of the fares would be the course adopted under like circumstances. Here, the lowness of price is less considered than the amount of comfort obtainable on a particular line, as well as the shortness of the time occupied by the journey. Thus the rivalry has taken the form of providing cars resembling that described, and thus it is that railway travelling in America is assuming the form of luxury tempered by accidents. The wonder is that more accidents do not happen. Many of the railways are single lines, hence the risks are multiplied as the traffic increases. The probability of a wrecked train being ignited by the burning embers

PULLMAN'S CAR, PACIFIC EXPRESS.

scattered from the stove adds another horror to the prospect. Still, when due allowance is made for all things, it must be admitted that the comparatively small number of railway accidents is very remarkable.

Meantime, the train has been speeding on its course

TRAIN-TRANSPORT STEAMER.

towards Chicago. Paris has been left behind, a place of which the name alone recalls the capital of France. More familiar to an English ear is London, with its river Thames and its Middlesex. At last Windsor is reached. This is the frontier town of this part of Canada.

The river Detroit separates the United States from the Dominion, and across it the train is transported on a large flat-bottomed steamer. From Detroit the journey is made on American soil through the State of Indiana and of Illinois. The country as seen from the window of the railway carriage is not prepossessing. The land may be very fertile, but it is certainly very swampy. Many of the farmhouses must be unhealthy places of abode. Contrary to Ricardo's theory of rent, the least valuable lands would appear to have been first brought under cultivation.

When Lake Michigan comes in sight, the objects that arrest attention are the sandhills, which, for a considerable distance, line its shore. These heaps and flats of sand give to the lake a maritime aspect, which the waves rolling shorewards tend to increase. Indeed, it is hardly possible to realise the fact of these huge sheets of water forming no part of the great ocean. The vessels which navigate them are to all appearance the same as the vessels which sail across the Atlantic, while the storms on these lakes are as terrific and disastrous as any which make the open sea the theatre of ruin and terror.

Finally, the train runs in front of handsome dwellings, which not only represent Chicago, but which line one of its most fashionable avenues. A man appears who sells tickets to those who purpose going by omnibus to an hotel, the price being half a dollar. He also takes charge of the luggage checks. By taking a check from him in exchange for that procured at starting, the traveller finds his luggage safely deposited at any address he may give. In this way much subsequent confusion and inconvenience are saved. At the station, a notice in a conspicuous place arrests the attention of the traveller. It is a warning against lending money to strangers. This excites a suspicion adverse to the sharpness, and favourable to the generosity, of the travelling public in America.

NEW YORK TO CHICAGO.

CHAPTER II.

CHICAGO.

BY the residents Chicago is often styled the "Garden City." Both its citizens and its admirers sometimes claim for it the still more dignified title of the "Queen City of the West," or the "Queen City of the Lakes." The pride they take in it is extreme, and the language in which they express their feelings is high-flown.

This appears quite natural to the traveller who has journeyed from England to the United States in order to witness the marvels which human industry and energy have wrought on the surface of the vast American continent. Books and newspapers may have prepared him for an extraordinary spectacle, yet neither tables of statistics nor any printed statements can enable him to realise the grandeur of the impression produced by a

stay, however short, in the modern city of Chicago.*
With a sensation of incredulity hardly to be repressed, he
listens to the stories which tell of the city's foundation
and history.

Forty years have not yet elapsed since the site of
palatial dwellings was distinguished from the surrounding
wilderness by a log fort, in which two companies of
soldiers were stationed for the protection of a few traders
who collected furs from the Indians in exchange for
trinkets. In those days civilised men regarded a visit
to the shores of Lake Michigan much in the same
light which many persons now regard a visit to the
sources of the Nile. Those who made the journey had
to brave the attacks of ferocious animals; had to face
the perils incident to an inhospitable and uncultivated
region; had to live in constant dread of an attack from
Indians more deliberately cruel than any beast, and more
crafty than any other enemy in human shape. The wild
men and wild animals have both disappeared.

The land which once yielded a precarious subsistence
to the hunter now repays the skilful farmer one hundredfold. Where weeds formerly throve in rank profusion, peach-trees are now heavy with precious fruit.

A city of palaces has taken the place of a few miserable
hovels. Similar transformations have occurred in other

* This chapter was written prior to the great fire which, in the
autumn of 1871, destroyed the greater portion of Chicago. Rebuilding is going on so fast that the city will soon be as striking in
appearance as it is represented in this chapter.

parts of the globe. Venice and Holland do not fall short of Chicago as evidences of what man can achieve in his struggle with rugged Nature and hostile elements. Yet the growth of either city was the work of many years,

TRADERS' QUARTERS, CHICAGO, FORTY YEARS AGO.

as well as of much toil; whereas Chicago has waxed great and famous within the memory of men still living, and not yet old. If another Queen Scheherazade were compelled to rehearse a tale of enchantment for the gratification of an exacting husband, she might find in the authentic story of the rise of Chicago materials which would produce a result as striking as that caused by a recital of the fabulous doings of Aladdin.

Although figures convey but an imperfect notion of

TRADERS' QUARTERS, CHICAGO, TO-DAY.

the wonders performed by the spirited and enterprising inhabitants of this city, yet, in default of a better medium through which to supply information, they must be employed. In 1830 the population of Chicago was about 100 persons, of whom a small proportion was white, the majority being black men and half-breeds. It was incorporated as a city in 1837, when the census was taken, and the number of inhabitants found to be 4,170. Ten years later the number was doubled; twenty years after its incorporation it contained 100,000 citizens, and at this moment the estimated number is 300,000. Nor

A HALF-BREED.

is there any prospect of a stoppage in the rate of increase. In every quarter hundreds of workmen are labouring at the erection of new houses, or the substitution of larger for smaller dwellings.

Nor is the rapidity of the city's growth more extraordinary than the way in which natural obstacles to its progress have been confronted and overcome. Situated on a low-lying part of Lake Michigan's shore, it was found to be very unhealthy. In order that neither damp foundations nor bad drainage should breed malaria in any of the houses, the entire business quarter of the city was elevated eight feet above its original level. This was done without interference with domestic comfort, stoppage of traffic, or injury to trade. While houses and shops were rising upwards, families slept securely in their beds, sat at ease in their rooms, took their meals as if the even tenor of their lives was undisturbed, while merchants conducted their daily business, and the public made their daily purchases.

For some years complaints had been made about the lack of good water for drinking purposes. The water supply obtained from the Lake was adequate in quantity, but was by no means wholesome. This was owing to the place from which it came being near the shore, and, in consequence of this, being contaminated with the sewage and refuse accumulated not far off. It was resolved in 1864 to remedy this defect by means of a tunnel carried under the water for a distance of two miles, and open at its farther extremity to the pure water of the Lake. Three years afterwards the new waterworks were in active operation, and they are capable of supplying 57,000,000 of gallons daily. Even this is hardly sufficient, and it is proposed to build a second tunnel. In addition to the supply from this source, there is a large quantity of pure water obtained from two Artesian wells, one of which is seven hundred and the other eleven hundred feet deep.

Another great work is the Washington Street Tunnel, an undertaking quite as noteworthy as the tunnel under the Thames, which used to excite the admiration of country cousins and intelligent foreigners. Finding that the amount of traffic in the Chicago River seriously impeded traffic over the bridges, which had to be opened whilst vessels were passing, it was determined to construct a tunnel under the river, and a short time after the project had been mooted the work was executed.

The rapidity with which Chicago has attained to the commanding position now held by it in the estimation of Americans, is due to the way in which opportunities have been turned to account quite as much as to any natural advantages it has enjoyed.

The situation is certainly a most favourable one. There is communication by water from this city to the Gulf of Mexico and to the mouth of the St. Lawrence. The lines of rail which centre here embrace fifteen trunk lines, and they run to every part of the Union.

Agriculture flourishes in the vicinity, and the farmer finds in Chicago both a market where his grain always commands a price, and a storehouse, whence he draws whatever he requires for the purposes of husbandry or for the comfort of his home. There is thus a continuous current of produce streaming through Chicago on its way to the consumer in the Eastern States or in Great Britain.

How speedily the trade in grain has been converted from an insignificant industry into an industry of unprecedented importance, let the following facts bear witness. In 1838 the shipments of grain were 78 bushels; in 1848 they were 3,001,714 bushels; in 1858 they were 20,085,166 bushels; in 1868 they were 67,896,760 bushels. If these figures did not appear in official returns of unquestioned correctness, they would be read with incredulity.

As it is, they excite wonder, and this is intensified when it is found that in other departments of commerce, such as the trade in cattle and lumber, the like progress has been made. Not long ago Cincinnati took the lead of every city in the Union as the place where the largest numbers of pigs were slaughtered, salted, and packed for exportation. On this account the city was commonly known by the name of Porkopolis. But, if the statements of the citizens of Chicago are to be accepted, the glory of Cincinnati has passed away, and the Garden City must henceforth be regarded as the one which lovers of bacon and ham are bound to honour.

The abundance, excellent quality, and moderate price of peaches, apples, and other fruit sold here in the autumn, excite the admiration of the visitor. In some streets the pavement is encumbered with boxes of fresh peaches. I learned that these are produced in the southern part of the State of Illinois. The soil and climate of that locality render fruit-growing as profitable there as it is in the southern parts of Germany. During the strawberry season five cars filled with strawberries arrive at Chicago daily. When the peaches are ripe, the supply sent to market every morning fills twenty cars, each carrying five hundred boxes of peaches.

Egyptian Illinois is the name of this prolific fruit-bearing region. Intersected by railways, the market is within easy reach of the cultivator's door. It is seldom that a crop fails, the climate being equable and temperate. Thousands of acres are still to be had by the settler. When I add that this land may be purchased for less than £2 the acre, I have said enough, I think, to excite the desire of many to possess and cultivate it.

Material prosperity and rapidity of growth have made Chicago a city of note, yet other things have made it a city of influence. Its newspapers are quite as remarkable and worthy of praise as its splendid streets and magnificent buildings, its extended commerce and public works. Among the magnificent edifices which, in different parts of the United States, are monuments of successful journalism, the office of the *Chicago Tribune* commands admiration. Situated at the corner of one of the principal thoroughfares, it impresses the beholder by the effectiveness of its architectural design, and this impression is not weakened by the fact that it is built of white marble.

As a newspaper, the *Chicago Tribune* exercises a vast and beneficent authority throughout the West. Its columns are singularly free from those offensive personalities which, in the United States, are too frequently considered the lawful weapons of the journalist. Its articles are at once pointed in tone and scholarly in style. A supporter of the Republican party, the *Tribune* is at the same time an energetic and astute upholder of free trade. It is the ablest representative in the press of that large and compact body of shrewd Western agriculturists which calls in question the justice of taxing the people at large in order to give the manufacturers of Pennsylvania and Massachusetts exceptional facilities for doing business on a large scale, and accumulating fortunes with unprecedented speed.

The *Chicago Times* is the democratic organ. Like its political rival, it is ably edited and well written. The *Chicago Evening Journal* is another of the more important newspapers. An attempt has recently been made to add a monthly magazine to the periodical literature of the Western States. The *Western Monthly* is well supported both by men of letters and the reading public. Judging from one point of view, it might be thought that in their feverish chase after wealth the citizens of Chicago had become indifferent to religious observances. Their favourite journals appear on Sundays as well as on the other days of the week. This is opposed to the practice not only of England, but of the Eastern States of America also. Yet while newspapers are in demand, the churches are not deserted. As a church-going people, the citizens of Chicago will bear favourable comparison with the inhabitants of any city wherein the forms of religion are rigidly observed. The churches are very numerous. Some of them are fine specimens of modern ecclesiastical architecture.

What a traveller values most in a strange city are good hotels, fine buildings, well-stored shops, and well-kept streets. In Chicago he will find all these things. The Sherman and the Tremont House are the principal hotels, and both are equal to the best hotels of the East. They both are on a par with other American hotels as regards the difficulty experienced by the passing traveller in getting a bed.

Throughout the United States and Canada the demand for hotel accommodation is one which seems to be insatiable and perpetual. On inquiry, the weary and astonished traveller learns that the state of things which gives him so much annoyance is the rule, that the revolving seasons exercise no influence on the huge and anxious crowd hurrying from one hotel and from one railway-station to another. At certain periods of the year an increase in the number of visitors to any American city of importance is perfectly natural. In the autumn it is customary for each State to hold its annual fair. These fairs, unlike those of the Old Country, have for their object the exhibition of the industrial products of the several States. The annual conventions, held for social and political purposes, likewise contribute to swell the throng of those who desire hotel accommodation. Another and exceptional gathering made the Chicago hotels crowded with visitors during my stay. A large party then stopped here on its way from California to the States of the East.

This party was no ordinary collection of excursionists bent upon enjoying a holiday and seeing sights. It was composed of persons taking to themselves the credit of being the pioneers of civilisation in California. Each one had gone to the Pacific coast in 1849, with a view to better his condition, and each boasted of having made California one of the richest States and brightest stars in the Union. The reception of this party was enthusiastic. The party itself was an illustration of the benefits conferred by the gigantic undertaking which supplied the link required to unite the Pacific and Atlantic with an iron highway. A printed list of the names and occupations of the excursionists gives evidence of their representative character. They had come not only from cities of note like San Francisco and Sacramento, but also from others less known to fame, such as Benecia and Stockton, Colfax and Elko.

Men of every position in the social scale had associated together to testify that they had laboured for a common purpose in bygone days. Newspaper editors, mechanics, farmers, carpenters, state senators, hotel-keepers, miners, policemen, druggists, shepherds, bricklayers, undertakers, merchants, and one artist, composed the motley gathering. The occasion was a memorable one, for it was the first on which the people of the Pacific had been brought into formal and fraternal contact with their brethren in other and remote parts of the continent.

The way in which the streets are kept is creditable to the city authorities. There is still room for improvement; yet, when the condition of those in New York is borne in mind, the streets of Chicago seem very good. Special and praiseworthy attention is shown to the safety of the foot passengers who cross over crowded thoroughfares. Policemen are stationed to see that the street is not monopolized by conveyances, to the danger and annoyance of pedestrians. These guardians of public order discharge their duty with an impartiality which merits praise. It is too often the custom, and in New York it is the rule, for policemen to be attentive to young and gaily dressed ladies, and to suffer all others to shift for themselves.

To quacks selling nostrums the police are not a terror. These charlatans ply their trade on the footpath in complete security, and with a success which is only too great. Among the crowd of poor labourers surrounding them they find credulous listeners and an easy prey. I saw one of these impostors doing an enormous business within a stone's throw of a leading hotel. His dress was that of a gentleman, and his manners and language were far superior to those of an itinerant vendor of the London streets. He had a pill which would annihilate every known malady, and an oil which would assuage every pain. As an inducement to buy the pills and the oil he presented the purchasers of either with an infallible cure for corns and bunions. This seemed to give satisfaction to his audience, for numbers exchanged their greenbacks for his rubbish.

Another branch of imposture flourishes here in the evening. In one street large numbers of mock auctions are publicly held. The business of many auctioneers appeared to be the same, that is, to sell watches and tell lies. Their energy and boldness could hardly be surpassed.

As the chief halting place between New York and San Francisco, the future of Chicago promises to be even more brilliant and extraordinary than its marvellous past. Its traders have already secured many new customers; its merchants have found new spheres in which to transact a lucrative business. To its markets additional supplies of valuable produce are now brought over the Pacific Railway. Thus the wealth of its citizens will increase with multiplied rapidity. Certainly those who live here must have much money at their command if they would enjoy the ordinary comforts, to say nothing of the luxuries of life. House rent is very high; clothing is very expensive. A married couple, whose income is £1,000, would hardly be numbered among the well-to-do citizens of this community. But, while the cost of living is great, the opportunities for growing rich are exceedingly numerous. None but the idle starve; none but the stupid die poor.

The Garden City is the paradise of the modern man of business. Compared with the bustle of Chicago, the bustle of New York seems stagnation.

ACROSS THE PRAIRIE BY RAIL.

ACROSS THE PRAIRIE BY RAIL.

CHAPTER I.

ST. LOUIS TO SALINA.

ON Thursday, October 23rd, 1871, I found myself on the Missouri Pacific Railroad, whirling to the unknown West.

I was seated in that most pleasant of inventions, a parlour car, where one can sit in comfortable arm-chairs, talk to one's companions, walk about, or in fact do exactly as one would in a pleasant little room.

On the 26th we woke up to the rolling hills and plains of Indiana, and breakfasted at Terre Haute. The country grew more level as we went on, and after passing some bluffs, we ran ten miles over a dead flat of rich alluvial land, and found ourselves on the banks of the Mississippi at St. Louis.

Like every European, I was prepared to be immensely

impressed by my first view of the " Father of Waters ; " but I must confess to a feeling of disappointment. I saw nothing but a very wide and very dirty river, covered with steamers ; a huge unfinished bridge ; and the city, looking rather dingy, with its long rows of warehouses on the other side.

Outside the cars when we stopped were six huge omnibuses, with four splendid horses to each ; and into these we all bundled, and drove down some little distance and on board a ferry-boat, where the omnibuses were drawn up side by side, the horses standing like rocks ; and so we crossed the river.

We had only a few hours here, and had not time to see much of the wonderful city, which some look upon as the future capital of the United States. Its rate of growth is prodigious, in the one item of railroads alone. Three years ago there were three, and now there are thirteen, running into the city ; and many more are projected.

After wandering about the streets hard by, and laying in a small stock of provisions, against our journey across the plains, we made our way down to the Depôt ; and were soon steaming away towards the setting sun.

Now began the really novel part of the journey. I was west of the Mississippi ; on that enchanted ground to which, if you have once set foot upon it, you must sooner or later return. "Mustang fever" is the name Westerners give to that wholly inexplicable feeling which is said to allure people back into the wilderness, almost against their own wills, when they try to cure

themselves of their roving tastes, by living in the cities of the Eastern States, or even in Europe.

Ere I went thither it was easy enough in my ignorance

DR. MILLER'S OFFICE.

for me to laugh at this theory; but now, I am not quite sure that I have wholly escaped the contagion. Certainly the journey of the first evening, as we left St. Louis, was most attractive. The moon was so bright, that I was tempted to sit up looking at the country till nearly every one else had gone to bed.

We ran for several hours alongside of the Missouri River, with the trees on its banks reflected clear and sharp in the smooth water, reminding one of some old steel engraving. Then crossing the river, we ran for some way with it on our right, and broken ground on the left; in some parts cultivated, in others forest, with deep gullies worn by water through the light sandy soil.

At last I packed up for the night; and woke about six on the 27th to find the train at a stand-still at some bit of a place, a perfect specimen of a mushroom town. It consisted of a few wooden houses, a saloon, a boot store, a dry goods store, and directly opposite our car the building in the picture, with a plate on the door, stating that this was "Dr. Miller's Office."

The ground was white with hoar frost; and the sun rose crimson over an open country, rolling away to the blue distance.

With joy I thought, "Only one night more, and we shall be at Denver;" but then, to my dismay, came the news that by some unlucky chance we had started in the wrong train, and must wait fourteen hours at Kansas City to catch the through train. My heart sank; for of all places to wait at, a more unpleasant one than Kansas City, which we reached about eight A.M., can hardly be found. But in a new country one has to put up with many little annoyances; so we determined to make the best of it, and drove up to the Lindell Hotel.

After a rather nasty breakfast in a very hot room, we went out and explored the town a little. It stands on a sandy bluff over the river; a strange situation to choose, as the foundations for all the houses on the slope have to be cut out of the sand at great expense and inconvenience.

There were two or three good streets, partly finished; several hotels; and scattered stores, some wooden and some brick, standing alone or in small clusters; little wooden saloons, with glass fronts, and various titles in English or German—"Colorado Saloon," "Denver Saloon," "Deutsche Gasthaus," &c.; and candy or fruit stores at the corners of what are in the future to be streets, but are now only masses of mud and stone with a boarded side-walk. One of these small booths bore a device painted in the very roughest style of art, of a large shoe, a green and red fly, and the word "syrup" written below them. After some reflection, I found that it signified that "Shoofly syrups" were to be procured here.

Along the river below the city are lines of warehouses, and one of the huge elevators for raising and shipping loads of grain. Of this curious process an excellent description may be found in Mr. Macrae's account of Chicago in "The Americans at Home."

After dinner, we went down to the depôt of the Kansas Pacific Railroad, to secure our tickets and places in the sleeping-cars. The heat was intense, the road being cut through sand-banks, which reflected the blazing sun overhead. The day wore away slowly, and I was rejoiced to hear about 10.30 P.M. the rattle of the four-horse omnibus outside the hotel, to take us to the train, and decided that I had seen enough of Kansas City to satisfy me; though I doubt not, from what I know since, I should have liked it better had I been less hot, and less impatient to get on.

At daybreak on the 28th I found we were on the Prairies in good earnest; and in a couple of hours we stopped at Salina for breakfast.

This was once a place of importance, as the temporary terminus of the line, where all goods were transferred from the freight cars to the ox trains destined to carry them through the dangers of a hostile Indian country to Denver and the towns of New Mexico. It then boasted a good many houses and stores, three billiard saloons, an ice-cream saloon, newspaper-office, school, and two hotels, besides fine streets marked out with stakes.

Now, as we walked up to the dining-room, a little distance from the track, it seemed the picture of desolation. There were, I think, not more than three buildings to be seen; one being the eating-room, approached by a shaky plank walk, and two small wooden houses. All the rest had disappeared; and the streets had relapsed into the original prairie, with no signs of cultivation around, save a scraggy rail fence, showing some settler's claim ground.

Directly we left Salina we came upon the regular plains; short grass in tufts on a sandy soil, and long stretches of brown, rolling away wave upon wave, like some great ocean turned into land in the midst of a heavy ground swell after a storm. Here and there was a prairie ranche or farm, with its coralle for horses and cattle, and the great heap of grass which represents the civilised haystack of eastern or European farms.

PRAIRIE RANCHE.

It is a lonely life, that of a rancheman. Settled out upon the prairie with his herd of horses and cattle, often without another house within a dozen or twenty miles, the only human beings whom he sees are the passengers on the daily train, or some passing emigrants, wearily crawling over the plains with their white-covered ox-waggons; except when he drives his beasts for sale to the nearest market.

In the winter the snowstorms are terrible; and in December, 1871, hardly more than a month after I crossed the plains, twenty-seven men were brought in on the Kansas Pacific Railroad frozen to death while tending their herds. One man, a large cattle-owner, was found dead thirty yards from his own door, with $5,000 in his pockets; having evidently wandered round and round, bewildered in the blinding snow, and dropped at last from exhaustion, not knowing he was close to his home.

But that people can live out on the borders of civilisation and prosper is a fact proved by the very existence of such States as Indiana, Illinois, Missouri, etc. Fifty— certainly seventy—years ago they were quite as wild and much more inaccessible than Kansas and the Territories are now.

I could not take my eyes off the country, so strange and new it seemed.

Suddenly my attention was attracted by a small brown post, about a foot high, planted in a sandy ring, with a little round pit in the centre. I looked again, thinking it a strange place for a post, and there was another, and a dozen more. All at once one of the posts threw itself flat down and disappeared into the pit, displaying four short legs and a twinkling tail; and I saw it was a prairie dog.

The fact was we were going through a dog-town, and

there the inhabitants sat by scores on their hind-legs praying at the train and rubbing their noses with their fore-paws. They are the quaintest little animals, and make charming pets, as they are very easily tamed.

PRAIRIE DOGS.

They are very falsely called dogs, their only claim to such a name being their cry, a short bark; but are really more nearly allied to marmots.

They are usually supposed to live in the strange company of a small owl and a rattlesnake; and I have heard people assert that in each hole these three most uncongenial friends are found. This fact, however, I have been unable to prove satisfactorily, never having myself seen either snake or bird with the prairie dogs.

Those who have had much experience in the West, tell me they have often seen the rattlesnake come out of holes in a dog-town, but have never seen any prairie dogs come out of the same hole.

The peculiar shake they give their short tails as they bolt down the hole has given rise to a western phrase, denoting great rapidity, " in the twinkling of a tail."

They are very difficult to catch, as their movements are very rapid. The best plan is to pour water down the hole, and so drown out the poor little beast, who comes up choking and spluttering, and is then easily made prisoner.

My brother M. had a narrow escape one day when drowning out prairie dogs.

His party was surveying in New Mexico, near Maxwell's; and being camped near a dog-town, they determined, one stormy evening, having nothing better to do, to catch prairie dogs. So accordingly, taking off shoes and stockings, and armed with tin pan, pail, and shovel, four of them sallied forth.

Turning a stream of water from the neighbouring irrigating ditch over the town, they waited over the holes with their hands down all ready to catch the unlucky little half-drowned dogs as they came up sneezing and snorting.

Two or three were caught and deposited in the tin pan with the lid down; but one large hole tempted them to further endeavours; and the water being properly directed down it, M. was all readiness to grip his prey, when suddenly, instead of the furry head of a dog, appeared the flat skull and glittering eyes of an old rattlesnake.

In an instant the valiant hunters were scattered, with the old rattler after them; and for some minutes a lively game was carried on, the rattler making darts at their bare shins as the four heroes hurled bucket, shovel, and volleys of stones against him. At last one lucky shot disabled him, and after he was dispatched they "concluded" not to hunt prairie dogs any more that day.

ACROSS THE PRAIRIE BY RAIL.

CHAPTER II.

SALINA TO COLORADO SPRINGS.

NEAR Brookville, a little station some way beyond Salina, we passed through a range of the bluffs, which one hears of so often as a feature of prairie scenery. They seem to be entirely water-worn. A smooth grass-covered slope rises up in a gentle wave from the prairie, and ends abruptly in a steep rocky face. Sometimes, nearer the foot of the Rocky Mountains, a few pines or scrub oaks find shelter on the rocky side of the bluff; but out here on the plains no twig was to be seen.

Among these bluffs large herds of horses and cattle were grazing; and we passed an occasional ranche till about mid-day, when every sign of civilisation was left behind, and we reached the edge of the buffalo plains.

Now began great excitement in our car, which was the last on the train; and some of us went out on the back platform to watch for the appearance of the buffalo.

This is not a very safe proceeding, as there is only a rail just across the end, and the sides are open. Still there is something pleasantly exciting in sitting there as one whirls along the single track, now over dry watercourses on fragile-looking trestle bridges; again between sandy banks, with high snow-fences to keep the snow in the winter from drifting and filling up the cuts; then over a wide smooth expanse, disfigured in many places by the long tongues of black running out on either side the track, where a spark from the "smoke stack," or chimney, has set the short buffalo grass on fire during the droughts of summer.

In some places these fires had run two or three miles over the country; and it was very likely owing to their pasture being so burnt that for a long while we saw no buffaloes alive, though endless skeletons lay on each side of the track, and we passed several dead bodies, in various stages of decomposition.

A most cruel and foolish fashion prevails on these trains, of shooting the poor animals from the cars as they go along, for the mere pleasure of killing. Of course, many more are missed than hit: but when they are wounded there are no means of stopping to dispatch them; so they die in misery along the line.

However, for some time it seemed as if the passengers on our train were not to have any opportunity of showing their skill; for we reached Fort Parker without seeing a buffalo. But suddenly we caught sight of two about a mile to the north.

Then the excitement among the passengers redoubled; in half-an-hour we heard the crack of a pistol from the front of the train; and as it sped on we came in sight of

CATTLE AND HORSES OF THE PRAIRIE.

three huge beasts, not more than two hundred yards from the track. They had been startled by the pistol-shot, and were galloping along in their clumsy way, parallel with the cars, as they always do when frightened.

They are most hideous animals, with heavy heads and shaggy shoulders quite out of proportion with their small hind-quarters. One wondered how such awkward-looking beasts could keep up such a pace; for long after we had passed them they kept in sight, still galloping after us, with their heads down.

The buffalo, or more properly bison, ranges over the great plains of Texas, Kansas, Colorado, and Nebraska,

PRAIRIE HORSES AND CATTLE.

in enormous herds; sometimes, in the summer, getting as far north as the 50th parallel. They seem very little disturbed at the invasion of their territories by railroads; and take kindly to the telegraph posts, evidently considering them put up for their special convenience to rub against.

This, as may be imagined, does not improve the insulation of the wires; and so many posts were rubbed down at first, along the Kansas Pacific Railroad, that orders were given to stick the new ones full of large and sharp nails. This, however, only made matters worse, as the buffaloes found the nails most charming combs for their shaggy coats, and the posts were knocked down more frequently than ever. So now the authorities have been obliged to give up in despair, and let the line take its chance.

At Elice we stopped for dinner. Then away we went again over endless plains, through blinding sun and dust; when, to my amazement, I saw here and there, to the south, beautiful lakes and rivers, with trees along their banks reflected in clear water. I had been assured that there was hardly any water, and not a single tree all across these plains; however, here they were most certainly, and I called my friends to look too. But as we approached one of the lakes it gradually faded away into the air, and we found it was nothing but mirage.

The utter desolation and monotony was only varied here and there by a herd of prong-horn antelopes, bounding away from the train, or a wolf skulking round some skeleton, or a great owl sitting blinking in the sun, or a group of soldiers or hunters drying buffalo meat, and curing hides at some " dug out " station.

These dug-outs were more used a year or two ago than they are now, as the Indians are quieter; but when the Kansas Pacific Railroad was building, and in the earlier days of stage-driving across the plains, they were absolutely necessary.

The following description of Pond Creek Station from "New Tracks in North America," will give a good idea of a fortified stage station :—

THE BUFFALO.

"Standing side by side, and built of wood and stone, are the stables and the ranche in which the drivers and the ostlers live. Behind is a coralle or yard, divided off from the plain by a wall of stones. In this is kept the hay, etc., belonging to the station.

"A little subterranean passage, about five feet by three, leads from the stables to the house. Another one leads from the stables to a pit dug in the ground, about ten yards distant. This pit is about eight to ten feet square, is roofed with stone supported on wood, and just on a level with the ground, port-holes open on all sides. The roof is raised but little above the general level of the ground.

"Another narrow subterranean passage leads from the house to a second pit commanding the other side of the station, while a third passage from the coralle to a larger pit commanding the rear. In both houses many repeating Spencer and Henry breech-loading rifles—the former carrying seven and the latter eighteen charges—lie loaded ready to hand; while over each little fort a black flag waves, which the red men know well means 'no quarter' for them.

"When attacked the men creep into these pits, and thus protected, keep up a tremendous fire through the port-holes. Two or three men, with a couple of breech-loaders each, are a match for almost any number of assailants.

"I cannot say how many times these little forts have been used since their construction, but during the three weeks (1867) we were in the neighbourhood, the station was attacked twice. The Indians are beginning to understand these covered rifle-pits, and the more they know of them the more careful they are to keep at a respectful distance."

About 4.30 we came across the buffaloes again. This time they quite fulfilled all one's expectations as to number; and till sunset we were never out of sight of them.

In one place we saw two hundred or more a mile away, and in another the plain was literally alive with a vast herd, three or four miles off, which I was told must have numbered some thousands. The groups near the track varied from four to twenty, of all sizes; and once I saw a little calf, with its father and mother galloping on either side of it, to protect it from the black smoking monster that disturbed their evening's grazing.

As the sun set in crimson glory over the plains, we reached the station for Fort Wallace. The depôt there was full of United States officers, who had driven in to get the mail and newspapers.

The Fort was too far off for us to see it in the twilight; but those we had passed in the day had given one a good idea of these little centres of civilisation, with their neat white quarters, and the welcome Stars and Stripes waving from the tall flagstaff, as guarantees of order and protection out on the desolate prairie.

I could hardly divest my mind of the idea that we should be attacked by Redskins, for the name of Fort Wallace is associated with such horrors; but we met with no worse a misfortune than a very bad supper, and sped on towards Denver.

During the night we passed Kit Carson, the scene of a terrible Indian raid in May, 1870; and Elko, from whence, in the day-time, Pike's Peak may be seen, a hundred miles away south-west.

A RAILWAY PASS IN THE MOUNTAINS.

Kit Carson is the point from which began one of the most marvellous feats in the annals of railroading. A hundred and fifty miles of road were wanting to complete the Kansas Pacific Railroad to Denver; and these hundred and fifty were graded and built in a hundred days. On the last day twenty miles remained unfinished. Double gangs were put on, working towards each other from both

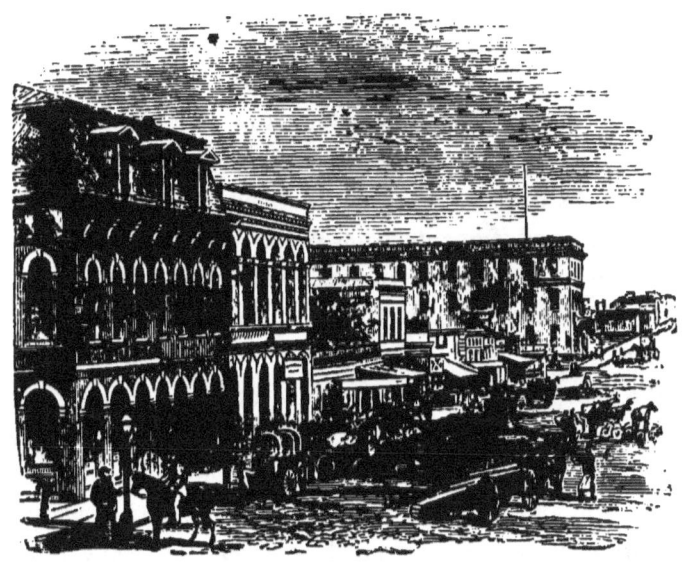

MAIN STREET OF DENVER.

ends; and before evening they met and put in the last rivet, one laying eight and a half, the other eleven and a half miles.

On the morning of the 30th, at six A.M., we steamed into Denver, where my brother M. was waiting for me on the platform.

Denver stands at the junction of the South Platte and Cherry Creek, about fifteen miles from the mountains. It is certainly one of the most successful of all the new cities of the West, and is growing at a perfectly prodigious rate. The streets are wide, and laid out in straight lines, crossing at right angles. There are very few "mean" or badly-built houses, such as one is too apt to see in a new western town; most of the business blocks are of brick or stone, and in the residence streets pretty wooden villas stand each in its own little garden plot. Cottonwood (white poplar) trees are planted along most of the streets, and seem to thrive. The stores are excellent; and if one does not object to paying four times as much as one would in England, all the necessaries, and most of the luxuries, of life can be easily procured in Denver.

We drove across the Platte to a sandy hill, which is to be in future the public park of Denver. It is called the Boulevard, and has a fine riding and driving road laid out, with four rows of cottonwood trees and irrigating ditches. This, however, must be seen, like many other things in the West, by the eye of faith; as at present the road is a rough, sandy track. When the Ute Indians visit Denver, they make the park their camping ground.

We got a very good idea of the city from the Boulevard. It looks just as if it had been dropped out of the clouds accidentally, by some one who meant to carry it farther on, but got tired, and let it fall anywhere.

For some miles out of Denver the railroad follows the

course of the Platte, till it turns to the mountains, and is lost to sight in the dark abysses of the Platte Cañon. Then, after leaving the Platte, the line follows one of its

AMONG THE ROCKY MOUNTAINS.

tributaries, Plum Creek (a " creek" in the West means any small river or stream), for about thirty miles, bordered with willows and cotton woods. The land on either side of Plum Creek is taken up by settlers, and fenced off into ranches for sheep, cattle, and agriculture.

Every mile took us nearer to the mountains; and at last the train began climbing up the Divide, or watershed of the Platte and Arkansas. Here we first got among the Pineries, a great source of wealth all along the Rocky Mountains; and at Larkspur passed a large steam saw-mill in full work. At length we stopped at the summit, beside a lake, which from its north end feeds the Platte, and from its south, the Arkansas.

This point of ground was 7,554 feet above the sea; only second in height as a railway pass to Sherman, on the Union Pacific Railroad, which is 8,370 feet.

Then began the run down to the Colorado Springs, about thirty miles. The road now was picturesque in the extreme, winding along the banks of the Monument Creek, past fantastic sandstone rocks, water-worn into pillars and arches, and great castles with battlemented walls, on the top of every hill. Through the pine-trees we now and then caught glimpses of the mountains, pink and purple, towering up ridge over ridge, till, about Husteds, the whole panorama south of the Divide lay stretched beneath us.

To the right the foot-hills rose, crowned by the grand snow-covered head of Pike's Peak, 14,336 feet high. To the south, the horizon was bounded by Cheyenne Mountain, standing right out into the plain; and from it to the eastward stretched the boundless prairie.

IN NEBRASKA.

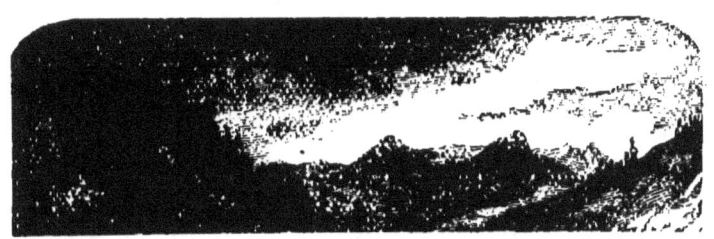

IN NEBRASKA.

CHAPTER I.

AMONG THE OTOES.

THE most important antiquities of the United States are the aborigines. Of their early history we know little, and the people themselves know less.

Notwithstanding their many prominent defects of character, the Indian tribes are entitled to the kind and considerate notice of a people whose sons are now fast occupying territories which, through ages, this strange people have owned with undisputed right.

The Otoes are a sub-division of the once powerful Dacotah or Sioux tribe. In May last, in company with friends, I visited their " Reservation."

Owing to the tide of emigration fast rolling over some of the lands once ranged only by the Indians, the authorities, in the interest of justice and humanity, have reserved to the Indians patches of country in which they may dwell undisturbed. These patches are usually selected by the tribes themselves; they are always ample, and consist of the richest, most favoured part of the country. In the possession and cultivation of these patches the Indians are faithfully protected and liberally aided by the United States Government. These patches are known as "Reservations."

The Otoes are of the well-known Indian complexion—a bronze red; the hair is long, lank, and jet black; the eye, in its ordinary mood, dull and sleepy; the brows are weighty; the lips ample and compressed; the nose is salient and dilated. The men are tall; the women, perhaps only by contrast, are short and dumpy. They usually live to a good age.

The Otoes' Reservation is a piece of land about ten miles wide, and twenty-five miles long, and for the most part in Nebraska; it is the finest portion of the State, being well watered by the Big Blue and its numerous and well-timbered tributaries; stone for building purposes in abundance, and the soil is unrivalled.

At the cost of the Government, one thousand acres of this country were broken up to give the people a start as cultivators. Aided by the Pennsylvania Society of Friends, the Government has also provided them with ploughs, waggons, harness, and all that industry could require. A store is established among them, from which they can obtain everything requisite at a

merely nominal profit. A school with efficient apparatus and well-trained teachers stands near to the Agency. A saw-mill is provided, where, to encourage them to live in frame houses, timber is cut free of charge. A grist mill is erected to grind their wheat into flour.

FOREST CLEARING AND WATER SAW-MILL.

Moreover, to all these provisions made for their personal comfort and the amelioration of their condition, in Major Green, the resident agent, is added a steady, personal interest. To their education, agriculture, and every part of the problem of the reclamation of this people, he brings all that can be brought by a shrewd and sympathetic mind.

Notwithstanding all this, however, the numbers of the tribe are fast declining. This large tract of land would seem to be a prison to them, and the costly service of a humane government a mockery. Their habits of thought appear fatally incompatible with civilisation. Be that as it may, as a matter of fact, the ploughed land grows nothing but weeds in rank profusion; the ploughs lie rotting and rusting here and there; the school is but thinly attended; the annuity paid to them by the Government is pawned to the storekeeper long before it is due; the grist mill is idle; there is no wheat grown for its stones to grind; and the saw-mill, which might be busy from morning to night, month by month, sawing up the finest logs of oak and black walnut, laying up wealth for the people, is employed for the requirements of the Agency alone.

Between the Otoe and the life of the modern world, unhappily, there appears to be no correspondence. In spite of every inducement and help, he prefers to live in his miserable and antiquated hut and wigwam, and longs to be emancipated from the miserable bondage of his present lot, to resume his wandering and predatory life, companion of the buffalo, the elk, and the deer.

On arriving at the Agency, we learnt that nearly all the chiefs of the tribe were actually at that time on a visit to the Cherokees, in the Indian territory, with a view of making a treaty which, if signed, sealed, and ratified, would result in the whole tribe exchanging life in the Reservation for their ancient life in the pathless forest and boundless prairie.

A MOUNTED DACOTAH CHIEF.

We visited a wigwam—the ordinary dwelling, built of sticks and bark. Having passed through the door, which was a suspended piece of skin, we found ourselves in a place dome-shaped, dark, and wretched, which looked more suitable for the occupation of pigs or bears than of human beings. In the centre was the fire, over which was a caldron, suspended by a chain from a tree fixed obliquely in the ground for that purpose. Immediately over the fire was a large opening, which allowed the smoke to go out, and the only light the dwelling had to come in. Several families occupied this one room.

Around this dingy, stifling habitation were the beds of the inmates, with the war-clubs and arms within easy reach. On the floor, near the fire, squatted two women embroidering, with beads, moccasins, and shot-pouches. Near to the woman lay a little child—a baby in fact—full length upon a board, to which it was fastened by the foldings of a cloth round its body and limbs, reminding one of a mummy. Behind its head was a strap, by which the mother could swing it on to her back or hang it up on the limbs of a tree. The child seemed very contented, and willing patiently to learn its early lessons in endurance.

From the city of the living we proceeded to the city of the dead. The Otoes' cemetery may be almost called the Otoes' place of worship. For this sacred place they have selected the highest piece of ground in the Reservation.

Their modes of burial are various. A coffin is always used; but sometimes they bury in an ordinary grave; sometimes their "burial" is upon a raised platform, and sometimes upon the branches of a tree. When a grave is made in the ground, it is covered with loose narrow boards, reared on end, like the ridging of a house, with an opening left for the supposed posthumous egress and ingress of the spirit; and food is placed near this opening for the spirit's nourishment. When the box containing the corpse is placed on a raised platform or upon the branches of trees, the food is hung up on the tree or placed upon the coffin. But whether the dead are buried in the ground or are laid to rest in a tree, the lid of the coffin is only tied down; it is never nailed. This arrangement is made in order that the supposed communication between the living and the dead, between the disembodied spirit and its old body, may be the more easily maintained. Animals and carnivorous birds feed upon the food thus exposed; but the Indian finds pleasure in believing that it is eaten by the soul of his departed friend in its supposed passage to and from its old yet still loved abode.

This tribe has a peculiar mode of sacrificing a horse in the funeral ceremonies of its master. The animal is shot whilst the grave is open; the tail is then cut off, and tied to a long pole; the carcase is then either deposited in the grave with its late master's body, or the skull is subsequently placed upon his grave. They do this in order to set free the spirit of the horse, believing that it will still be useful to its master, and will carry him through the land of shadows and serve him in the anticipated happy hunting-grounds of his aboriginal paradise.

During the evening, in one of the largest wigwams, we were entertained by lithe young girls and boys of the tribe dancing around the fire their peaceful dances. The chicken and the sheep dances were selected, and were accompanied by hideous music of drum and tambourine, and the singing of the older men and women. In the morning we had observed the sluggish interest the boys had manifested in the school duties, under the tuition of a pretty Quakeress; but now they were gay and active, with motion in every limb. Now and again one of the number would be punished for not doing his duty, by being tied like a horse by the master of the ceremonies to a pole of the lodge; yet the dancers danced well and in good time, far into the small hours of the morning.

Some of the peculiar traits of these wild people cannot fail to commend themselves to the civilised traveller. The simplicity of their eloquence has challenged the admiration of all those who have made their language a study; nor have any people ever evinced higher principles of devotion to what they believe to be cardinal virtues. Faith has furnished the Christian martyr with motives to sustain himself amid the horrors of the stake, but the North American Indian has endured the keenest torment of fire without the consolation of the gospel. His belief in a system of gods in the elements is mistaken; his conceptions of the duties of social life are wrong; doubly wrong are his notions of death and eternity; yet he proves himself to be possessed of many of the best sensibilities of the human heart. He exhibits, in great strength, those ties which bind a father to his children, and link whole tribes together in the bonds of brotherhood. In helpless ignorance, he lingers by the dying couch of his relative with sincere and clinging affection; and his loving memory of the cherished dead ceases only with his life. No costly tomb marks the place of burial, yet the affectionate, dutiful, and oft-repeated visits of survivors to the last resting-place of those whom they loved when in life, conciliate the respect and sympathy of civilised and Christian nations.

What does it appear must be the destiny of this ancient people? From all the facts of the case, I have a strong yet melancholy conviction that they are doomed to extinction. In spite of all that has been done and all that can be done, as a people they must pass away. It may be urged that they have a possessory right to the soil; but they neither claim nor can they use other rights than those used by the buffalo and the deer. It has been said by men who had given their lives to the study of the problem of Indian life, "Keep the Indians on their worn-out hunting-grounds, surround them with settlements, and the savage hunter will be forced to become a tiller of the soil. The way will also be opened for the introduction of the arts and sciences, and the benign influences of Christianity." But by favourable experiment this has been proved to be a mistake. Surrounded by civilisation, and by all inducements to its occupations and attainments, they see no good in them. Restless instincts—instincts common to them and to the wild herds they slay—pine for the wild life, and it is clear the wild life they must have or perish.

They possess no power of progress. Under these circumstances in a progressive world, extinction seems to be inevitable, but the conditions of a civilised life bring on the ultimate fate with accelerated speed.

It is a fact, too, that they will not embrace the religion of Christianity. Is not their doom therefore anticipated in the solemn records of inspiration, "The nations and kingdoms that will not serve God shall perish?"

IN NEBRASKA.

CHAPTER II.

THE PRAIRIE ON FIRE.

I HAD not been long settled in my new home when a fire swept over a vast portion of the State (Nebraska), crossing the plot of land on which I had settled.

My house, stable, and barn were built of "lumber," but in a substantial manner, and with a view to permanency. The stable contained a valuable pair of horses, and the house was comfortably stored. Near to the stable, in stacks, stood one hundred tons of hay which had been laid by for winter use. My family consisted of myself and a man and a maid-servant.

Around the whole I had had the usual fire-break ploughed, though in taking this precaution I half felt that I was only following a needless custom. Within the break was abundance of long, dry grass which the summer had grown and the early winter frost had killed. The day after the ploughing of the break, the mowers were intending to clear it. Accordingly they came; but, the day being Sunday, I could not allow them to go on with their work. I believe that it is no mere arbitrary law of God that we should rest on Sunday; a rest-day is the real want of the body and soul. So, determining in this wild and solitary place to start straight on this matter of Sunday-work, I sent the men away, with the request that they would return on Monday.

At about three o'clock on the very Sunday afternoon, a man in breathless haste descended from a panting horse at my door, opened it, and without introduction, broke in, with the tidings that a vast fire was burning to the windward, and in a few hours more it must be on us. "Take a few things with you and clear off to the creek. Into the water, and stop there till it's gone by. That's your one chance."

And within the time that it takes merely to write these sentences, this dreadful herald had pronounced them, re-mounted his horse, and was off again, doubtless on a similar startling but merciful mission to other settlers.

I had scarcely had time to realise the full import of the message, or to recover from the utter bewilderment into which, by its nature and suddenness, I had been plunged, before additional and more certain warnings arrived. Falling ashes, which had been carried up by the flames, and borne far ahead of their course by the stiff breeze which blew from the direction of the fire, announced the terrible truthfulness of the horseman's words. At first their fall was here and there, like the big solitary drops of thunder-rain; then thicker and faster; now they fell cooled; then they were still warm; then hot, and finally glowing red. With these changes the temperature of the heated air painfully increased. The stiff breeze became a breeze of fire, and momentarily increased in strength.

Now the heavens darkened; up from the south-east stretched, like a canopy, dense clouds of smoke. Above they were dark; but their darkness deepened as they neared the horizon. The horizon itself was brilliant with a long, quivering band of vivid crimson.

In the direction of the approaching destroyer, and not far from us, lay a low line of hills, behind which, for some time, its terrible glowing was hidden. As the fire neared this line of hills, their outline darkened, their golden background became more intensely brilliant. Suddenly, at point after point, the flame reached their tops; speedily the top at all its point was in a blaze, and the whole range rolled down what appeared like floods of burning lava. Then the flaming hills mingled with the flaming, smoky sky. Fire ran along upon the ground. Fire leapt up towards the clouds. Miles to the east, and miles to the west, there was one unbroken line of swift-marching fire. Against this terrific belt of light, distinct objects which lay between us and it—hay-stacks, neighbours' cattle, solitary trees, even fence-posts— loomed out near, huge and dark.

Meanwhile we loosed the horses, and turned them out to take their chance, and busied ourselves as our friendly horseman had advised. We carried down to the creek

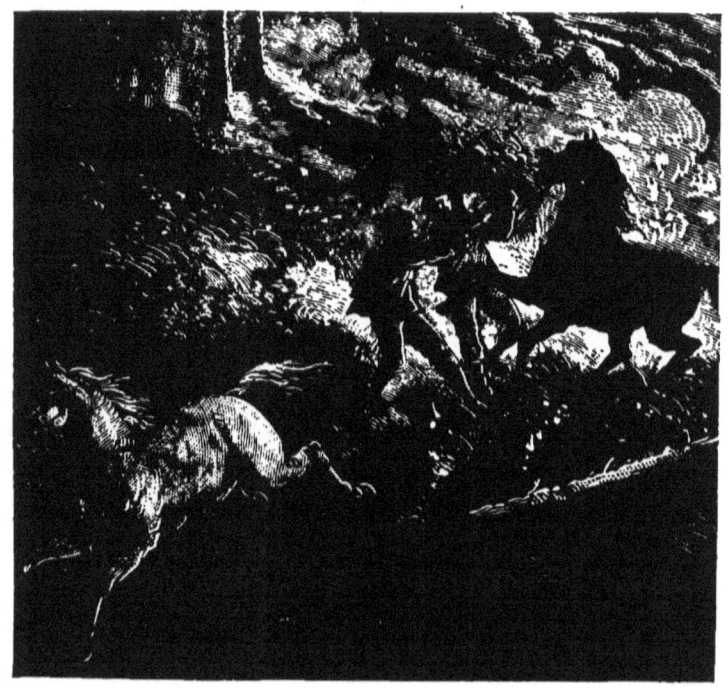

HORSES AND THE FIRE.

in portmanteaus, bed-linen, blankets, and a few other things such as we should require for the coming night. But we had scarcely had time to reflect on the most desirable things to save before our projects were stopped, and we were forced to look after our bare personal existence. Whilst the flames were still a mile away, it seemed as if we, and all around us, must catch fire by the mere heated wind; so much so, that all bodily action was rendered impossible, indeed the mere effort to breathe was exhausting, and we had to be content with a very small provision for the future wants of our possible existence that night. It is wonderful how little a man feels that he really needs when life is at stake.

At length actual fire about us began. Flying embers ignited the patches of grass here, there, and everywhere. Then the heat of the last few moments, which it had seemed impossible to survive, became by contrast coolness itself. The deafening roar, which for the last hour had increased, now became what nothing seems to express so well as the prolonged boom of near cannon. We dragged ourselves into the water, and with the little strength we had left, forced under everything we would preserve, and stood ourselves chin-deep. Now I closed my eyes to protect them from the dreadful scorch. The exposed face seemed to be actually in flames, and death by drowning or suffocation seemed the only alternative presented, and choice must be immediate. Instinct chose the former.

*　　*　　*　　*　　*

How it happened after the plunge under the stream I know not. But, owing to the sparseness of fuel for the fire in the immediate neighbourhood of our refuge, the terrific crisis lasted probably but a few seconds; how many, I have no grounds even for conjecture, save that we just lived through it, though only just.

The fire passed on; and we left our refuge to lie upon its scorched banks, too exhausted and too oppressed with gratitude to realise the ruin it had wrought. The house was still burning, stable and hay-stacks were still burning; but the remotest idea of attempting to save them never entered my mind, nor the mind of my servants. I was abstracted from everything by a dreamy, thankful amazement at my own existence. Before night set in, house, stable, and stacks were mere smouldering heaps.

Gradually the fire patches, which, after the main body of the flame had passed, still lingered around us, burnt out, the air cooled, and the now seemingly bitter wind revived me. I took in at a glance our new condition, and gave my first unselfish thought to wondering what might be the fate the poor horses had met.

From the smouldering desolation, in time I turned away to look at the still burning fire. Miles away to the north-east, it seemed to be raging with unabated fury and breadth, presenting even a more awful glory, seen from this its smokeless side. One could almost admire it now, freed as one was from the terrible and absorbing anxiety of contemplating its threatening approach. It pursued its onward march as an army in battle array— lines and columns of fire, bearing banners of flame, moving with the precision of veteran regiments under inspiring and resistless commanders. Here and there

THE REFUGE IN THE PRAIRIE FIRE.

small detachments lingered in the rear of the main body to finish their terrible work of vengeance.

The night advanced, and with its advance receded the flames, till in the early morning nothing was seen but the black line of its march.

My catalogue of loss is brief. It consists of one word, and that word is *all*. Hundreds of my fellow-settlers must have suffered in like manner. When the fire had passed me, an almost boundless prairie lay before it, nearly the whole of which was covered with grass, dry and long and rank, tempting it on and on like trains of gunpowder the travelling spark. As one took one's last look at it, the misery of one's own lot was aggravated a hundredfold by remembering that all that night, perchance all the next day, and indeed until a change of wind may be, which might mean nights and days to come, the flames would be gathering upon our fellowmen as they had just gathered upon us, strewing their dreadful path with smouldering homesteads, ruined families, and may be human dead.

IN COLORADO.

M

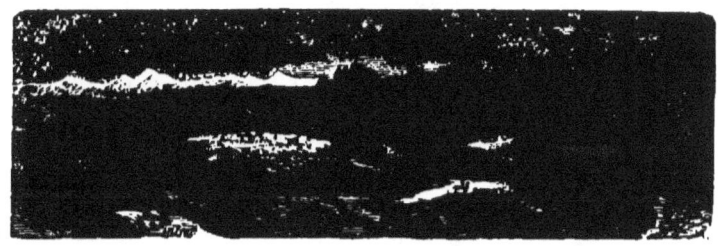

IN COLORADO.

CHAPTER I.

AT COLORADO SPRINGS.

YOU may imagine Colorado Springs, as I did, to be in a sequestered valley, with bubbling fountains, green grass, and shady trees; but not a bit of it.

Picture to yourself a level, elevated plateau of greenish brown, without a single tree, sloping down about a quarter of a mile to the railroad track and Monument Creek (the Soda Springs being six miles off), and you have a pretty good idea of the town-site as it appeared in November, 1871.

The streets and blocks were only marked out by a furrow turned with the plough, and indicated faintly by a wooden house, finished, or in process of building, here and there, scattered over half a mile of prairie.

On the corner of Tejon and Huerfano Streets stood the

office of the Denver and Rio Grande Railway, a small wooden building of three rooms, in which all the colony work was done till the new office should be finished; and next to it was my home. It was a wooden shanty, sixteen feet by twelve, with a small window of four panes on each side, and a door in front.

OUR SHANTY.

Over the door M. put up his tent, with a rough board floor, which served for our sitting-room by day, and he slept in it at night. The shanty was lined with thick brown paper, so that it was quite air-tight; and though it had only been ordered on Thursday, and finished on Saturday, was really quite comfortable. In one corner we put my little camp bed; in the other my trunks.

Our furniture had not arrived from Denver; so M. found an old wooden stool, which had been used for mixing paints upon, tacked a bit of coloured calico over it, and deposited upon it a tin basin; and there was an impromptu wash-hand stand. A few feet of half-inch board were soon converted into corner shelves; and, with warm red and yellow Californian blankets on the bed, and a buffalo robe on the floor, my room looked quite habitable.

In the tent we put the stove, a couple of wooden kitchen chairs from the office, and a deal table, while M.'s bed by day made a comfortable sofa.

Our days went on this wise. Up at seven A.M. in the cold frosty air, with thick ice on the bucket of water, a walk of nearly half a mile took us down to the restaurant at eight, with a fine appetite for breakfast. Our food at that important meal was good and plentiful. Beafsteak or venison, biscuit (the American name for hot rolls), hot buckwheat cakes, eaten with butter and molasses, and the whole washed down with bad tea or excellent rich milk.

At 12.30 daily the train came in, and we went down to dinner, and saw all the new arrivals, some coming to stay at the Springs, others only stopping for an hour before taking the stage for Pueblo, Maxwells, or Santa Fe, in New Mexico.

It is a sight I am never tired of watching: the coach with its four splendid bays, standing in front of the office; the horses held by two men, a third with the reins ready;

the "messenger" stowing his mail-bags safely away; the passengers bundling in for a period of misery of varying length. When all is ready, and not till then, out walks the great man, in yellow blanket coat, and hat securely tied down with a great comforter. He mounts the box, arranges himself leisurely; the messenger is beside him, wrapped in buffalo robes; then the reins are put in his hand, and as he tightens them, away go the horses with a rush that takes one's breath away.

The Western stage-driver, on his box, with the "lines," as they call the reins, in his hand, is inferior to no one in the Republic. Even the President, were he on board, must submit to his higher authority.

Among many and varied accomplishments, these stage-drivers have the credit of being able to consume a prodigious amount of whisky. The following story is the most remarkable illustration of this trait in their character; the incident occurring, I was assured by the narrator, on the mail that runs south from Denver to Santa Fé.

"As the coach drove up to the door of the hotel in Denver, out stepped a jolly-looking Englishman, and asked for the box-seat. The stage-driver eyed him from head to foot dubiously, till he saw in his baggage a keg of whisky, when, with a slight change of countenance, he told him, 'he guessed he could fix it.' And when the messenger cried 'All aboard,' the Englishman and his whisky took the box-seat.

"The first twelve-mile stage was monotonous, the

Englishman probably meditating on four hundred and fifty miles by coach; and the stage-driver, who seemed desperately taken up with his horses, on 'that thar whisky barrel.'

"The station is reached at last; and the Englishman, feeling cold, announced that he was going inside for the next stage; but wishing to do the right thing, asked the stage-driver first whether he would have a drink.

"'Waal,' says he, 'guess I will,' and catching hold of the barrel uncorks it with a masterly hand, and for the space of some twenty seconds goes through an elaborate process of 'star-gazing' through a wooden keg.

"'Waal,' he remarks, 'that's rale good,' setting it down.

"'Oh, if you like it,' says the Englishman, 'just keep it up there, I shan't want any for the next stage,' and jumping in, dozes off in a troubled sleep, or at least the nearest approach to one which the bumps and jerks of the old Concord coach will allow, till they change horses at the next stage.

"Feeling thoroughly chilled, he jumps out and asks the driver for the keg, which is handed down to him, and through which he proceeds to 'star-gaze' in the most approved Western fashion. To his surprise and horror not a drop oozes out.

"'Why,' he says, 'what's gone with the whisky?'

"'Why,' says the stage-driver, 'ain't there none thar?'

"'No,' said the Englishman; 'what's happened to it?'

"'I guess it leaked out.'

"'But that's impossible; where can it have leaked to?'

"'Waal,' says the stage-driver, 'guessed it's leaked down my throat.'

"'Down your throat! why, man, you don't mean to say you've drank it all?'

"'Why not? thar warn't much whisky nither.'

"'Why, my good man, you don't mean to say that in a twelve-mile stage you drank the whole of that keg of whisky?'

"'Yes. But then, ye know, what's one keg of whisky amongst one stage-driver?'"

The first few days passed quickly in learning the ways of the country, and settling down in our new life. Up to that time I had seen nothing at all alarming in the way of Indians or wild beasts; but there came a day when M. was obliged to go up to Denver on business, leaving me under Mr. N.'s care.

The day was busy enough. I had to manufacture a cage for some snowbirds which the French nursery-gardener had caught for me; and when one has nothing handy to make a cage of, it naturally takes some time.

Leroy caught the cock first, late one evening; and I kept it all night in a little pen on the top of my trunk, made of "Martin Chuzzlewit," a candy box, my travelling bag, and two blocks of firewood; the whole covered with a bit of flannel. But next day came the hen; and, of course, the two must have a cage, and the cage required much thought. First I begged an old candle-box from the grocery store, and over the front of it I twisted some wire which the darky from the office got for me off an old broom-handle. As there was not enough to finish it, and none was to be bought for love or money nearer than Denver, I had to put a board over the rest of the opening.

In the evening, however, when I secured the tent flap, and set to work to make up my fire, I began to feel rather creepy, though I was but half-a-dozen feet from the office, with plenty of protectors there. My only living companion was a very dirty black-and-white kitten called "Tucker;" but M. had left me his revolver, so that I felt pretty secure, and when I was well warmed I locked myself in my room, and with the pistol close to my side, and the kitten on my feet, was fast asleep in a minute.

How long I had slept I knew not; but I was awoke by a sound I had never heard before. Peal upon peal of demoniac laughter, mingled with shrieks and screams, seemed sweeping past the shanty—now loud, now softer, till they died away in the distance. I flew up, and with the revolver across my knee, listened in a perfect agony of terror; but the sound, whatever it was, had gone by, and by the time I had struck a match, and found it was four A.M., I knew what it must be—a band of Coyotes (prairie wolves) had come through town on a raid after stray sheep.

And small blame to me if I was frightened; for many

a stout Westerner has told me how, camping out on the plains in hourly expectation of an Indian attack, a band of Coyotes have made every man spring to his feet with rifle or revolver cocked, thinking the wolfish chorus was an Indian war-whoop.

We agreed to pay a visit to the Soda Springs at Manitou, six miles off, where there was a temporary hotel, kept by English people; so we set off about five P.M., in a good carriage, with rather a wild pair of horses. It was dark, except for the light from four inches of snow, against which the road showed quite black, while an icy north wind whistled round and through us. The road there will give some idea of roads in the new country.

Up to Colorado City (a gambling and drinking den two miles from the railroad), it was two or three inches deep in stiff mud; but it was beautiful, compared with that beyond the city up to Manitou.

We had to cross the Colony irrigating ditch two or three times, besides Camp Creek, and various other creeks, on bridges made of loose planks laid crosswise over supports without any fastening or any railing at the side.

But worse still was the ford over the Fountain Creek, close to the Soda Springs. We drove straight down the bank into the river, which boiled and foamed over a rocky bed, and the descent was so steep that when the horses were in the water the hind heels were as high as their backs. We plunged and struggled through and up the other bank, and then breathed freely. Next day, when I abused the road, I was seriously reproved by some stanch Coloradian, who said it was as good as any one could want.

The wooden hotel at Manitou was a thorough new-country hotel. Being only built for summer visitors, the boards had large spaces between them; and on waking in the morning I was surprised to find how much daylight showed through the outer walls of my room.

The night was cool, to say the least of it; and, in spite of five blankets and a bear-robe, whose weight almost suffocated me, my face was nearly frost-bitten.

When I looked out of window I found we were in an exquisite valley, with pine-covered mountains rising five thousand feet from La Fontaine qui Bouille, as it used to be called in old trapping days, now it is merely Fountain Creek. The sun shone bright over the snow; and blue jays, with crests erect and screaming voices, flashed through the scrub oak.

The springs lie in a group along the stream, some on the bank and others in its actual bed. There are four principal ones. The largest, "The Navajoe," has formed a large basin, six or eight feet across, in the centre of which the water boils up ceaselessly, and the overflow runs down to the creek by a tiny channel thickly encrusted with soda deposit.

Some of the smaller springs are chalybeate; and the water of the Fountain, the clearest and most delicious I have ever tasted, is strongly impregnated with the mineral waters of the springs in its bed.

A road leads out of the upper end of the valley over the famous old "Ute Pass," where the Ute Indians of the mountain lay in wait for the mountain buffalo coming down to feed in winter on the plains, when driven out of South Park by the snows.

All this little valley and the town site of Colorado

THE UTE PASS.

Springs have witnessed terrible fights between the Utes and the Cheyennes. It was a kind of neutral ground; and when one tribe dared to set foot upon it, their enemies were all ready to pounce upon them. So late as 1869 the Cheyennes scalped and killed six white people between the present railroad track and Colorado city.

While we were at Manitou Dr. B. took me up my first Cañon (pronounced Canyon). I can best describe this most curious feature of the Rocky Mountains by saying what I saw.

We turned off the road near the hotel up a track through scrub oak, wild gooseberries, raspberries, and rose-bushes. The valley at first was merely a common wooded mountain glen; but suddenly we found ourselves in front of a narrow gateway of rocks one hundred or more feet high, and in a moment we were in the Cañon.

The trail led up the bed of a little stream now dry, which had sawn its way through walls of sandstone of every imaginable colour, from rich purple and crimson to salmon-colour and white. The rocks were worn into the most fantastic shapes, battlements, and castles, and pillars, hundreds of feet high. Sometimes they opened out enough to allow the growth of splendid Douglassii, R T, under which we passed. One tree had fallen, and we had to walk up its stem covered with slippery snow; and then came a sudden twist, where the rocks almost met overhead, sandstone on one side, limestone on the other, and I touched both sides of the Cañon without stretching my arms to full length.

It was the wildest scene: the towering rocks, black pines, white snow, and no living thing save ourselves and a solitary hawk wheeling round against the streak of blue sky we saw above our prison walls. For a while we went up twisting and turning every twenty yards, so that looking back one could not imagine how one had got in or would get out again.

This Cañon at the time I saw it had never been properly explored; but some adventurous spirits had been up it for several miles, and said the scenery grew grander and wilder the farther you went.

As far as geologists have been able to work out the subject, the Cañons are made simply by the action of streams. Every stream in Colorado, from the tiny mountain rill to the Arkansas and Rio Colorado, has its Cañon in some part of its course; and in the case of the latter river, the "Big Cañon" of the Colorado is two hundred and thirty-eight miles long, and its walls rise up vertically from the river to a height of from two thousand to four thousand feet.

After a while, the new office of the Fountain Colony was finished, and to my real regret I gave up my poor little shanty, and settled in a plastered room behind the office, which was in the upper story of one of the principal dry-goods and grocery stores of the town. But the weather soon made me glad to be in a tolerably well-built house.

As an illustration of the extraordinary changes of temperature to which this place is subject, an event on the 18th of November will serve. The evening was so fine and warm, that we all took a long walk down to the Santa Fé road. Two hours later, however, a violent snow-storm came on, with wind; and by breakfast-time next morning it was blowing a perfect hurricane, the

A COLORADO CAÑON.

house rocking so that sometimes we thought it would go over.

The cold, as we ran down to breakfast, was fearful; and, notwithstanding innumerable wraps, my right ear, which was on the windy side, was in such torture I thought it must be frost-bitten; but I was consoled for the pain by learning that when it hurts you are all safe, and only when a nice comfortable sensation of warmth comes on are you in danger of being "frosted."

Dinner-time brought no abatement to the storm. The snow was drifting tremendously, the strong wind lifting the dry, powdery particles right off the ground, and blowing it across the plain in clouds of white dust. The thermometer registered 13° above zero.

In the middle of dinner the unearthly screech which in America stands for a whistle, announced the arrival of the train; it had come through the snow-drifts nearly up to the top of the chimney. The wheels, and every ledge and corner, were a mass of snow, and the icicles hung in a crystal fringe along the boiler.

The snow, towards evening, began to disappear; next morning the sun was blazing, and not a breath of air stirring.

The town grew every day; not a week passing without some three or four new buildings being completed.

Mrs. P. had organized a capital school, which for the first three months of its existence she taught herself, and had as many as twenty-five scholars. And as the population increased, it was determined among a few members of the colony to try and set on foot a reading-room where the young men might spend their evenings. So one night they called the colonists together, and we carried chairs, benches, and lamps over to the railroad office, and had a capital meeting. One hundred and forty-three dollars were subscribed on the spot, and in three weeks the reading-room was open.

IN COLORADO.

CHAPTER II.

ITS CELEBRATED SIGHTS.

THE "Garden of the Gods" is one of the sights which every one must see who comes to Colorado Springs; so we drove up there one bright day, in the ambulance, with our two brown mules, Pete and Baby.

An ambulance may be best described as a wooden tray, with two seats on springs, and a canvas top. It is a very good conveyance for the rough roads of the West, being very light, and easy to manage—so light, indeed, that in a violent wind-storm, one day, M. was turning to go into the stables, and a gust caught him in the act, and blew the ambulance right over.

The road turned off to the "Garden" about four miles up from Colorado Springs, on the way to Manitou, and first led us across a field, and then to a bridge over the

Fountain. It was just wide enough for the waggon (in America all kinds of carriages are called waggons), and

GATE OF THE GARDEN OF THE GODS.

was quite rotten. How we got over I know not, for, in the middle, Pete, who had been turned out to grass for some time, and was not on his best behaviour, shied violently. However, we did get over in safety, and drove along what was dignified by the name of a road, but it more resembled newly-dug celery trenches, varied by gravel-pits, and a deep ditch right across every few hundred feet.

At last we got to the outer garden, a great open space of grass, with scattered pines, and here and there fantastic sandstone rocks; and further on, to our right, lay the great rocks, the real wonder of the Garden.

First, we passed a number like weird figures praying, with their heads all bent towards Cheyenne Mountain; then a red sandstone nun, with a white cowl over her head, was trying not to see a seal who stood on his tail, and made faces at her. There, I was told, two cherubs were fondly kissing, though to my eyes they looked more like a pair of sheep's heads; and so, finding new absurdities every moment, we came to the Great Gateway, and driving between the rocks, two hundred and fifty feet high, we turned to see the view.

The great rocks were a warm salmon-colour, with black pines growing in their crevices, and bringing out the richness of their colouring, and between them, as if set in a glowing frame, shone Pike's Peak covered with snow, and Cameron's cone and the foot-hills, all blue, white, and pink, three or four miles off.

We had come into the Garden the back way; but the best plan is to go first through the Great Gateway, and drive out at the other end. Driving back the way we came, we got along without misfortune till we reached that horrid bridge; and this time Pete positively refused to cross. Twice M. got him to the middle, and Pete tried to push poor Baby over the side, and then backed sideways. At last we got out, and M. took them at it four times; but a mule's mind, when once made up, is not to be moved, and we had in the end to drive round

A COLORADO BRIDGE.

another way; and on the whole, perhaps, Pete was right, for he had twice gone through a bridge—the last time having been lamed for a month by it; and he doubtless thought the chances were considerably in favour of his going through this one too.

To the north of the Garden, among the foot-hills, lies Glen Eyrie. It is a very beautiful valley, about half a mile across, into which debouches one of the finest Cañons in the neighbourhood.

One evening the moonlight looked so tempting that five of us determined to explore the high ridge which divides Glen Eyrie from the Upper Garden.

Passing the Echo Rocks, and making them sing two or three songs a couple of bars behind us, a narrow track led us to the top, with a scramble, and once there the view was superb. To the right, on the crest of the hill, were a group of pines, through which the moon shone so brightly it was like white daylight. Behind us lay the Glen, with its red rocks, and the hills rising up to old Pike, all covered with snow; and in front of us another deep valley, shut in with a high rock wall, widening out above into a park, and below narrowing into a Cañon which apparently had no exit. None of us had ever been there before; but we plunged down the hillside through deep snow, with here and there a Spanish bayonet (*Yucca*) sticking up to prick the unwary, and down to the bed of the Cañon.

The Cañon was so narrow that only one person could squeeze along between the rocks at a time; and I began seriously to fear it would soon get too narrow for us to turn round and escape, and that we should have to stay there for the rest of our days. Suddenly, however, out of the intense black shade, we came into a streak of brilliant moonlight, which streamed through a cleft in the rocks before us, not more than three feet wide; and we saw the outer valley in dazzling light beyond.

We were well repaid for our scramble, and there certainly is a great charm in a new country in feeling that one is looking upon places which probably none have ever seen before, save some stray trapper, or savage Indian.

At the end of November we had what is called a "cold snap," and for a day or two the thermometer got as low as 9° above zero. It soon passed off, bright sun and warm days following it; but its effect was to drive large herds of antelopes in from the plains to the shelter of the bluffs.

One day, hearing they were near town, we had out the ambulance, with the mules, and drove off in search of them, armed with a revolver.

We had not gone more than a mile and a half west of the town site when we saw a herd in a hollow to the right of the road. M. got out and crept away after the antelope, telling me to drive slowly after him. There were about twenty-three, and when we had crossed the hollow and got to the top of the next rise, we saw an immense herd of some hundreds a mile west. I watched M. along the crest of the hill, the antelope meanwhile running round below him out of sight, when suddenly he stopped.

Piff, piff, piff went the pistol, and I drove on to him. No luck, alas! as Butler, the negro at the office, had loaded the revolver, and carefully put in half charges; so every shot fell short. We drove after them, and M. got three more long shots from the waggon, but to no purpose.

Next morning by seven o'clock we were off with Mr. de C. in the waggon to try after antelope again; and I tried to cure my uncontrollable dislike of firearms by keeping one of the rifles on my knee till it was wanted.

We fell in with two herds in the same place as yesterday; but our luck was as bad as ever, for so many parties

HUNTING THE ANTELOPE.

of shooters were out after them, that we could not get within range. We drove on the bluffs in hope of smaller game, and Mr. de C. got a "cotton tail" rabbit (*Lepus Artemisiæ*), and we looked in vain in the bushes for prairie chicken.

But we got what quite repaid us for the want of sport

—a magnificent view of the mountains to the south, which at the town are hidden by Cheyenne Mountain. Across long stretches of plain we saw the Greenhorn jutting out from the main chain, with the Spanish Peaks sticking up blue and golden beyond it, and in the furthest distance the Raton Mountains, over Maxwells, two hundred miles away.

The antelopes were so starved that winter that they came in by thousands off the plains all along the base of the mountains.

At Greeley, the colony town north of Denver, they came among the houses and got shot from the windows. A herd of forty was crowded in a field, and the Greeleyites went out and surrounding it shot them all down. It seems cruel to kill them in this unsportsmanlike manner.

Another of the "sights" of Colorado is Monument Park.

About twelve miles north of the town lie a set of bluffs, the beginning of the Divide, running out from the mountains some twenty miles into the plains, and forming a series of grass valleys or "parks," as they are called in the West.

Monument Park is a large glade about two miles long running from east to west; the end of the glade being filled up with the blue and red walls of the foot-hills covered with pine-trees, which rise about three thousand feet above the valley. The south-western slopes of the bluffs are covered with the Monument rocks, which, at first sight, strike one as irresistibly absurd.

MONUMENT PARK.

They are of every height and size, from the great giant thirty feet high, to the pigmy of twelve inches; sometimes they stand alone; sometimes in groups of twenty

MONUMENT ROCKS.

or more. No two are alike, and each year they change their shape; as wind, snow, frost, and rain go on with the work of destruction, with which for ages they have been moulding this group, as if over some set of Titanic graves.

The New Year came in with bright sun, no wind, and doubtless sky.

In the morning a swarm of Indians had come into the town. They were Utes from New Mexico, and M. recognised many old acquaintances among them. There were several squaws of the party, whose ugly faces we were glad to see, as their presence is a sure sign of peace ; and for a few weeks previous, there had been rumours flying about of an intended outbreak among the Utes on the other side of the foot-hills.

The men and women were dressed very much alike ; except that the women's hair was cut straight round just below the ears, and the men wore their long scalp locks, with little cases of beads (like a bouquet holder) surrounding them. Some of their faces were painted with red stripes, and one had red and yellow stripes on the cheeks, yellow being the second mourning for a near relation.

When an Indian dies, the nearest of kin paint themselves entirely white, and retire to their lodges for ten days, during which time no one sees them. They then come out and paint themselves red and yellow till the end of the month or moon, when the days of mourning are over. The Ute war-paint, which I did not see, is black and white.

The Indians were intensely interested in the railroad track—the first they had ever seen—and squatted down,

ITS CELEBRATED SIGHTS. 191

rubbing the metals with their fingers. Some went up to

UTE INDIANS.

Denver by train, and the rest camped up the Fountain,

about a mile below Manitou, and hunted in the mountains.

Two days later I saw their lodges, made of skin, supported by poles, as I drove the L.s up to the Soda Springs; and one of the tribe was kind enough to scare the rather wild ponies I was driving, by standing in the bushes close to the road, with bow and arrow ready drawn. Horses, and still more mules, cannot bear the smell of an Indian, and will often "scare" at them, as the phrase is, when their driver cannot see one within a quarter of a mile.

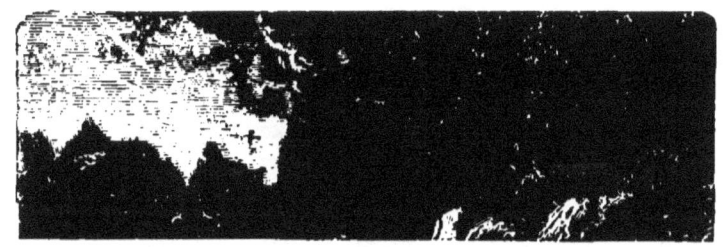

IN COLORADO.

CHAPTER III.

OVER THE RATONS.

WHENEVER I get out on the plains and look southward to those endless mountain ranges which stretch away into New Mexico till they are hidden by the roundness of the earth, I am seized with a longing to go south and see them. But the stage journey is enough to deter any one from going who is not absolutely forced to go. My desire, however, was not thoroughly cured till M. gave me an account of a night-journey he made across the Ratons. I think it will give you a good idea of the difficulties of winter travel out here.

"We're going to have rough work over the mountain to-night," I said to Dutch Sam, the messenger of the S. O. M. (Southern Overland Mail), at the Red River

Station, where we stopped for supper on a night in the end of December, 1870. "Who takes us over?"

"Frank Blue's turn to-night, I think. — Supper's ready."

In I bundle, and find Frank stretching himself, after a three hours' snooze, preparatory to driving forty miles on a bitter winter night over the roughest piece of road in Western America.

"Hullo, where are you coming from? Who's aboard?"

"Nobody but me."

"Bully for you! Where's your bottle?"

A "square drink" opens his eyes a little, and as we discuss some steaming beef-steaks he gives us the pleasant news that "the other side" (the north side of the mountain) was sloppy with half-melted snow as he came over in the morning, and that it is probably now a sheet of ice.

"However," he adds, "as there's nobody but you aboard, don't much matter if we do go over."

At which I thanked him, and asked him how long ago it was since he had overturned, so as to calculate the chances against his doing so to-night.

"Well," he said, "Old —— went up with me last night, and I told him the mules wanted roughing. He said they didn't, so just to show him they did, I piled the leaders into a heap just above Dick Wooten's there, and I guess from the row the insides—Old —— among 'em—kicked up, he'll believe me the next time."

"But where on earth did you go?" I asked.

"Oh," he said, "I waited till I got a snow-bank kinder handy, pulled on my near leader, slipped my brake, bucked myself into the snow-bank, and let the old shandydan rip."

"Well," said I, "thank goodness *I* am not one of the Company's officers!"

After another long drink we muffle up, and I jump on to

the box-seat beside Frank, while Sam turns inside for a snooze.

In five seconds more the helpers swing the leaders into their place, and with a tremendous plunge that threatens to burst every piece of tackle about them, the four mules "lay themselves down" and race away, their ears laid back along their necks, their tails tight down to their quarter, bucking and squealing along the only piece of level this side of the mountains. We are over it in a minute, and in and out of the dry watercourse with a lurch that makes me grip the handrail, the mules steadying on the further side, where begins the steady pull up the first ascent.

What a gorgeous wild scene it is!

In front the range rises in a black weird wall, and the full moon streams down on the white broken crags, making them look like the battlements of old ruined castles; and across the road the pines shed a ghastly shadow, setting off still more brightly the moonlight on beyond. And now we are in the cañon itself, and the crags beetle a thousand feet high on either side, save where here and there a long steep slope runs up far into some snow-covered glen.

I express a hope that the other side is as clear as this one, as up to the present the road has been perfectly clear of snow; and Frank says that all is dry up to the summit, but from that down we shall catch it.

We trot on in silence for the next half-mile, crossing and re-crossing the stream several times, till we open a little glade, at the further side of which we see the camp-fires of a Mexican bullock-train, whose ten waggons are drawn up in a semicircle against the rock, forming an enclosure to keep the cattle from roaming. The fires shed a warm

FISHER'S PEAK.

kindly blaze round, lighting up the dark pine stems, and playing on the little white points of rock at the opposite side of the cañon. The team object strongly to passing them; but Frank's heavy whip soon reassures

Kitty, one of the leaders, who squeals and bucks each time the thong cracks across her quarter.

As we lose the fire we plunge again into the darkness of the cañon, and steady the team as we near the Devil's Gate, so called from two enormous rocks through which the watercourse has worn a channel only just wide enough for a waggon to get through, and which tower over our heads to some two or three hundred feet high. It is a wild place, and was famed in old times for desperate Indian encounters.

From this up to the summit we have better going, and the mules, well warmed to their work, take us up quickly and steadily; and almost before I am aware a piercing cold blast warns me that we have reached the summit, and that there is nothing to shield us from the north wind, which I see swirling the snow in wreaths on the top of Fisher's Peak, ten miles away. Anxiously we strain our eyes down the northern slope, only to find deep snow over everything.

The road turns sharp at right angles along the crest of the hill for the next quarter of a mile past the old tree which marks the boundary-line of the territories of Colorado and New Mexico, and on which ten years ago a famous highwayman was lynched. As we reach the turn in the road where the descent begins, we pull up and begin to prepare for it.

Sam and I get out and tie the front and hind wheels together with ropes so as to block the coach entirely, and prevent the hind-wheels from swinging round, as, if they did so, it must upset the coach.

This done, Sam goes forward a little way to reconnoitre. Not five steps has he gone when his heels fly up

THE ROAD AT THE SUMMIT.

into the air, and down he comes on the broad of his back, with a crash that re-echoes through the still night; and it is some seconds before he can find breath to reply to our questions of what had happened, and how did it look. All that we get, however, is a confused sentence, out of which I catch, "The darn'dest meanest road this side of ——," which we receive with shouts of laughter, and Frank tells him to jump on board.

This time I get inside, as Frank says he's "going to run 'em down."

Sam follows my example, and we each station ourselves at a window. Frank gets the team's heads straight, and in another second we are sliding over a sheet of ice at twelve miles an hour, on a gradient of one foot in ten.

A sudden jar, a grunt, and a half-choked groan from one of the mules, while a half-smothered curse from Frank tells that something has happened. I crane out, and see the off-wheeler down flat on her side, fortunately with her legs outward, as, had they fallen inwards, she would have thrown the other wheel mule, and then nothing could have saved us. As it is, how we get down the next four hundred yards goodness only knows; but at the end of it we find a big snow-drift; and into it Frank unhesitatingly shoots us, thus enabling him to stop the team.

I run to the leaders' heads, while Sam gets hold of the fallen mule, and now the question is, how to get her on to her feet. Frank tells me to swing the leaders across the road from the mule so as to give her room to struggle; and then applying the whip as hard as he can across her loins she struggles up, only to fall again, as the leaders, frightened at the crack of the whip, make a wild plunge forward. My feet slip from under me, and for a second I think that the whole team and the coach beside are over me; but, thanks to the rough lock of the wheels, they could not move the coach, and I struggle up, only to have the same thing happen again.

But this time the old mule keeps her feet; and after cutting away the snow a little round the wheels, we jump in, and off we start again.

The worst part is over; and the next half-mile we sail along grandly, when down goes the same wheeler again, and we drag her thirty or forty yards before we can stop. We get her up again; but she is so much hurt and cowed by the fright, that she falls again three or four times before we reach the station about a mile ahead. Here we find that the poor brute has not got a single hair on her left side from the point of her ear to the root of her tail, and on the shoulder, ribs, and hip-bone a good deal of skin has come off as well.

"But any way," Frank says, "she's only a mule;" and sure enough a year afterwards, I sat behind her over the very same piece of mountain, looking as if she had never skated down the Ratons.

You will easily imagine that after hearing this story I felt somewhat like the man who said, "I *kin* eat biled crow, but I don't hanker arter it," and did not "hanker" any more after a journey across the mountains.

A MERCHANT OF THE FAR WEST.

A MERCHANT OF THE FAR WEST.

CHAPTER I.

ADVENTURES.

IT was a magnificent autumnal evening. Our ship was covered with canvas towering to the very truck; her studding-sails spreading outwards like the wings of an immense sea-bird, and herself "staggering," as the sailors say, under a fresh quarter-wind, with as much as she could carry, neither less nor more.

The horizon was clear—a rare thing at sea—and gave promise of a glorious sunset.

We were in the middle of the Atlantic, and not a sail in sight; so that we seemed to be the living centre of the whole visible world—of the ocean which swept around us, and the blue dome of the cloudless sky that descended over us, resting its huge rim upon the circumference of the plain of waters.

The passengers had finished dinner, and were pacing the deck; or, broken up into little parties, were singing, telling stories, reading, or gazing over the bulwarks upon the ruddy rays of light becoming more intense in the western clouds that gathered round the setting sun.

Such delightful evenings on shipboard always spread a happiness throughout the whole vessel. Sickness and moroseness are both banished; and those who ordinarily "dwell apart," become frank, affable, and communicative.

It was so with one of the passengers, whose appearance and manners had arrested my attention ever since we had left harbour. He was a man of ordinary stature, and of a light wiry make. There was something peculiarly striking in his countenance, yet one could hardly tell what that something was. The features were all small and well formed; the complexion dark and swarthy; the hair lank and jet black; the eye—yes, therein lay the mysterious *something*.

For four days I never heard that man open his lips.

He sat during meals at the corner of the table near the door of the saloon, nearly opposite to me, and separated always by a considerable gap from his next neighbour. He seldom raised his head while eating; never partook of more than one dish, and of that very sparingly, eating very rapidly, and never drank anything stronger than water; so that his meal, begun always late, and taken in silence, was over in a few minutes, and his seat again empty.

When on deck he paced up and down from morning till night, speaking to no one, and apparently absorbed in his own thoughts. His step was as peculiar to himself as were his other manners; short and rapid, and noiseless, like a wild beast speeding onwards towards its prey, he seemed to glide along the deck.

But no one could look at that face without feeling there was something behind it "out of the common." That eye! How quickly it glanced round, and seemed to fasten on everything and everybody; now changing to calm sadness, brooding in deep thought; or suddenly—one knows not why—becoming fixed with a sharp piercing glance of fire, beneath the contracted eyebrows, as if it gazed upon a spirit; while the nostrils were distended, the lips compressed, and the features lighted up with deep emotion.

A total stranger myself to all the passengers, I could not make the inquiries which I felt prompted by curiosity to make, about this unknown person. But one day after dinner—on that beautiful autumnal evening I have described—two passengers beside me, while conversing about the great emigration then taking place from the United States to the shores of the Pacific, happened to forget the name of some dangerous pass.

"What *is* the name?" exclaimed a Yankee, stamping his foot with irritation, and knitting his brow.

"Jonada del Muerto between Chihuahua and Santa Fé," said the unknown one, without lifting his eyes or speaking another word; then rising from his seat, he proceeded to the deck as if he had uttered something in a dream.

"Queer chap that!" remarked one of the speakers, as he gazed after him; "I knew *he* knowed it, if man did."

"Who is he?" I inquired.

"Well, I expect," said the Yankee, "that he does some business in the far west. I heard a St. Louis man —that tall, red-haired fellow at the other table—say, that his life would be one of the *loudest* in any language, if it were in print."

This description, peculiar though it was, made me desire a closer acquaintance with the stranger; and, accordingly, I was soon on the quarter-deck beside him, and after a few distant and cautious approaches, based upon the state of the weather, the appearance of the ship, and prospects of the voyage, etc., I managed to come so near him as to ask, alluding to his remark in the cabin, whether he had travelled far in the west?

His answer, expressed in quiet and courteous language, prompted other questions; and these led to replies and counter-questions, until hour followed hour, and the gorgeous sunset was hardly noticed, and the rush of the waves was unheard, and the heave and pitch of the vessel unperceived, and the whole scene around me became as a dream.

My companion was one of those characters to which an island like ours can no more afford room than a crib in the Zoological Gardens can afford scope to the camel or antelope for the display of their endurance or swiftness.

His life, in its several features, may be very briefly stated.

He was a German, well born, and connected with at least one noble family in Scotland. He had early left Europe to "push his fortune" in America. Partly from a love of adventure, and partly from the hope of opening up a new line of trade, he had, soon after landing, travelled across the continent, and penetrated north to the Columbia River, and south to Mexico and California. He ended by purchasing some mules, loading them with merchandise suited for sale or barter; and taking a few intrepid spirits with him to share the dangers and profits of his enterprise, he commenced a regular business, which had increased upon his hands, until at last—after fourteen years of great success and singular endurance—he was eminently "the merchant of the wilderness."

His plan of operations was this:

He had thirty waggons, each waggon having attached to it ten to twelve mules, guided by two men, dead shots, armed with rifles. Their caravan, therefore, consisted of about three hundred and fifty mules and sixty men.

"Now, suppose these waggons loaded with merchandise, purchased chiefly in Manchester, and worth many thousand pounds," I asked the merchant, "what was the journey which they pursue?"

"Why, I'll tell you," was his reply. "It's *rather* a

long one. Starting from New York or Philadelphia, I go right across to Ohio—sail down the river to the Mississippi—up the Mississippi to St. Louis— from St. Louis up the Missouri to Fort Independence, four miles inland ; and there we all meet and begin our real journey *in earnest* to the west."

"Pray, how far must you travel before beginning what you call your *real* journey ? "

"Oh! not far—only across the United States, and down one river and up another—let me see—perhaps about two thousand miles."

A pretty long introductory start, thought I.

"But whither," I asked, "after your start from Fort Independence ? "

"Twenty miles," he replied, "bring us across the Indian lines, and then we are clear of the settlements. Our course lies almost due west by south, for about a thousand miles across the prairie, until we strike the river Mora, ninety-five miles east from Santa Fé. Passing a spur of the Rocky Mountains, called Taos, I divide my company ; sending thirty of my best men with the half of the goods along the Rocky Mountains, and as far as the Columbia, to trade with Indians and trappers for their furs. This journey occupies about six months. I proceed myself with the second division due south for about twenty-one hundred miles more to Durango and Zacatecas."

" And how long does this journey take ? "

" I leave Fort Independence in the month of April, and

A CARAVAN IN CALIFORNIA.

reach Santa Fé in about three months; and in six months more I am back to Santa Fé from the south on my way home. For fourteen years I have been altogether only about three years in the settlements. I have constant travelling each year at the rate of about six hundred miles a month."

Such was the route of the merchant of the wilderness. Perhaps some of my young readers may endeavour to trace it on a map? It is something like a journey!

Space would fail me to recount a tenth of his strange adventures and hair-breadth escapes.

The mere physical strength required for such a journey is immense. He and his men, during the twenty-four hours, had never more than two and a half hours of sleep; and were obliged to supply themselves with food by hunting the buffalo, or killing any game they chanced to meet. They cooked on fires made from the dry dung gathered from the grassy prairie, and lived for months without bread or vegetables.

It is seldom that such visitations can be provided against. Two or three years before I met the merchant, he had been placed in circumstances which demanded all his courage and decision of character. They occurred somewhere near the Rocky Mountains, and during one of those sudden and heavy falls of snow which he has once or twice encountered in his journey, and which lasted for *five weeks* at a time.

The cold at this time was extreme. After toiling some days through the snow to reach a river, the whole company got so benumbed and downhearted, that a halt was called by one of his men, who had, on more than one occasion, exhibited a tendency to rebellion. They all refused to go farther, though the river was within marching distance before sunset, if they put forth all their energies to gain it.

The plan of the mutineers was probably to desert the waggons, and go off with the mules. I forget now the details of the story. But I well remember the description he gave of his feelings, when he found himself hundreds of miles from any settlement, in the presence of sixty determined men with loaded rifles, and on the verge of mutiny. He knew that not a moment was to be lost. So, going up to the ringleader, he commanded him to mount and proceed. On his refusal, the merchant drew a pistol and shot him dead! He then went to the next, and gave the same command. The mesmeric power of fearless determination and authority was felt, and the whole band proceeded.

He took the first opportunity of explaining all his reasons to them; and while they admitted, after their danger and sufferings were over, that he was right, and had saved their lives, he insisted upon giving himself up to justice when he reached the States. Being freed from blame, he then petitioned Congress for a law to regulate such authority as his in the wilderness.

"Were you not afraid of your life?" I asked.

"With sixty rifles against me," he replied, "my life was easily taken. Either of us must succeed. If they did so, we must all have perished; if I did so, we were safe: I was like the captain of a mutinous crew at sea."

What firmness, courage, and self-reliance from a sense of right!

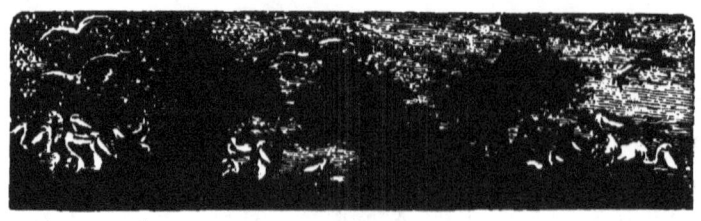

A MERCHANT OF THE FAR WEST.

CHAPTER II.

ADVENTURES.—(*Continued.*)

ONE of the most singular escapes of this adventurous merchant took place during his last journey home.

From some unknown cause, probably the flooding of distant rivers—the prairies often become like a shoreless sea, full of scattered green islands, which mark the more elevated knolls. One morning, he and his band found themselves on such an island.

"We had just reached," he said, "Prairie Fork, two hundred and fifty miles from the nearest settlement at Fort Independence. The creeks were full. To proceed with our mules, for even a few miles, was impossible. Most of my men would have been drowned. Fortunately, they had a large quantity of buffalo meat, and from the space of ground which was dry, and the probability of the water somewhat abating, food could be obtained for the mules. But the settlements *must* be reached to get assistance, or all might perish. I resolved to make the attempt on foot.

"Taking a small quantity of buffalo meat with me, I started alone, committing myself to the care of God; for it was a terrible journey, such as I never had to encounter before, and never can again. I once rode with three mules eight hundred and twenty miles in eight days, yet that was nothing to this journey!

"The water had risen forty feet in some places. After almost every mile of dry ground or shallow water, where I could wade, I was obliged to swim some creek or deep gully. One night I swam six large creeks. The cold was also great; yet, by God's help, I travelled the two hundred and fifty miles in twelve days. I could not have slept more than two hours in the twenty-four, and then it was a sort of feverish dose in my wet clothes, on a prairie knoll.

"For the last four days I had not a particle of food, and was compelled to eat, or rather to gnaw, my leather moccasins and braces. My clothes were almost all torn from my back. To add to my sufferings, I strained my ankle, and for the last hundred and ten miles—wet, naked, famished—I dragged myself along with great agony. I at last reached the end of my journey, dreadfully swollen; and for six weeks I was confined to bed.

"Assistance was sent my men by a large escort with

light canoes. With the loss of many of my mules, they at last arrived, but took *five weeks* to perform the journey. Thank God, I saved them! But it was worse than even the Jonada del Muerto."

I was told that this adventure had attracted great

INDIAN ATTACK UPON A MERCHANT'S CAMP.

notice in the United States at the time, though I never met any account of it. I believe it was strictly true.

Another "peril in the wilderness" is from the Indians. The Blackfeet and Raphoes are the deadliest enemies to the white man: no distance will weary them.

The merchant arranged his camp every night in preparation for an attack. The waggons were drawn up in a double van; the mules and men in the centre; while a watch was placed outside. If the alarm was given, his men with loaded rifles ranged themselves under the protection of the waggons, and thus their position was almost impregnable. Often, however, in a desperate attack, they came to hand-and-hand struggle; but though occasionally some one of his men was killed, they came off always conquerors in the end.

A ludicrous incident occurred in one of these engagements.

One of his men had been scalped by the Indians some years before, and survived, as very few have ever done, the terrible operation. He procured a wig when at the settlements, and again was in a *scrimmage* with the savage foe; and again the knife was ready to encircle the head whose hair was seized by the Indian, when, lo! the whole scalp came away of its own accord, and the bald head lay shining on the grass!

The Indian looked horror-struck. Expecting to meet a foe, he was persuaded that he had met a magician, and dropping both the wig and his tomahawk, he fled with a yell from the field of battle, leaving the enemy in possession of his precious life, and of his precious peruke, with the tomahawk to the bargain, as a trophy!

Some of the Indian tribes are all cavalry regiments. The *Cumanchoes* are a splendid race, numbering many thousands. They are all beautiful riders, women as well as men, and their hair being permitted to grow until it reaches far down their back, waves gracefully in the wind as they charge at full gallop. Their ease on horseback, the singular rapidity and agility of their movements, can only be equalled by the most practised riders. This moment they sit erect, in the next they are invisible.

While charging, they stoop down, and draw the bow on the right side of the horse's neck, but, suddenly stopping, the horse is wheeled round, and nothing is visible but a part of the foot of the rider; his whole body is now hanging down on the other side of the horse, and his existence is discerned only by the arrow that comes whizzing from the unseen foe. The practised rifleman often shoots through the horse's neck to hit the Cumanchoe's head, which he knows to be on the other side.

So chivalrous are these Arabs of the western desert, that they often give warning of their intended attack, that there may be a fair stand-up fight. I may add, that they are all teetotallers.

But the Blackfeet! These are the black snakes in the grass. The poor trappers have singular escapes from them. Unless I had perfect confidence in my informant, the facts which he related, and which others have since confirmed, of what some men are capable of enduring while effecting their escape from these wolf-like pursuers, seem altogether incredible.

"Well," said the merchant, "it *is* wonderful! Such a fellow as Kidcarstens, for instance—"

"Who was he?" I asked.

INDIAN MAN AND WOMAN MOUNTED.

"Oh! a famous half-bred, who all his life was among those wilds. Kidcarstens was once roused up by four warriors of the Blackfeet, who had vowed to kill him, as he had scalped one of the tribe in battle. They came on him as he was trapping on the North Fork, more than two hundred miles from Taos. I know the spot well. He had nothing for it but to throw away his precious rifle and traps, and run for his life. He did so, and Jack *could* run, I assure you; he was all small bone, with muscle like whip-cord. He never stopped, ate, or slept, till he reached Taos; and then he was only a few miles ahead of his foe. He stopped to drink in crossing the streams; that was all he had during the terrible race!"

"A race of two hundred miles! impossible!" I exclaimed.

"Longer, sir,—longer, I believe; I have taken three days to the same journey on horseback, at the rate, I calculate, of more than seventy miles a day. No man who knows the Blackfeet and Kidcarstens would doubt it. *They* beat most runners; but Jack beats all!"

"Talking of escapes from Indians," he continued, while he burst into a hearty laugh—a rare thing for my singularly grave friend, who seemed often to have caught the statue-like composure of the Redskin—"the best I ever knew was old *Peg-leg Smith*. We called him Pegleg because he had a wooden leg. He trapped along the Rocky Mountains, and sold to me, or to the Hudson Bays, at the mouth of the Columbia.

"Peg had a white horse—his only companion for

many a long day. His weapons were a long bowie-knife, and a rifle that never missed; but powder and shot were more precious to him than gold or diamonds. He knew the haunts of the Indians and their habits so well, that he managed generally to keep out of the way of unfriendly tribes. But once on a time either Peg was out of his way, or some roving Blackfeet were out of theirs, and so they spied him, and he fortunately spied them. Well, I need not tell you that the white horse was soon put to his paces, to gain the nearest but yet distant settlement of friendly Indians.

"Away went Peg, and after him went the Blackfeet, with a yell that might have made any man but an old trapper give up in despair. Miles were soon passed, until the savages were a good way behind, and sometimes out of sight; but he knew well that, once on his trail, they would run along it, without a halt, like bloodhounds, ay, weeks after he had passed; for these fellows can follow up the trail of a deer even six weeks after he has gone over the ground, and can detect his track, however frequently crossed by others; and, in the end, run him down! Poor Peg's horse left a surer impression behind than the deer! The enemy was coming on.

"Once dark, he thought he would cheat them, and arrive among his friends before daybreak. But the old horse was becoming wearied. The sun had yet a good yard or two to descend. On he went, however, for some miles farther, always keeping a good look-out towards his rear, till on reaching a height, he saw two of his enemies far off, but other two very close upon him, in full cry; so that it was evident they must very soon come up with him, more especially as he had entered on a mountain path.

"What was to be done? A few minutes more and they must be on him!

"He first unslung his rifle. He must risk one shot at all events, though but one more remained in his pouch. He made another preparation, which I shall tell you of immediately. Halting on a rising knoll, he dismounted, made his obedient horse stand like a statue, and calmly waited the approach of the two Indians, who must suddenly appear round a sharp turn, towards which he pointed his unerring rifle.

"Suddenly one of the enemy rushed on the path with a cry of surprise, and, in a moment, lay dead. The other appeared in a second after, when Peg-leg, having unstrapped his wooden leg, flourished it over his head; then presenting the stump to the foe, he flung the wooden leg at the Indian's head! But the savage, seeing his companion dead at his feet, and seeing, too, as he fancied, a *real* leg coming towards him, he stood for a moment panic-struck by this exhibition of witchcraft, and springing out of sight, was seen no more.

"Peg reached the settlement in safety, with his leg under his arm. The other Indians, he afterwards learned, had been warned by their companion to retire with all speed from the great wizard.

"Poor Peg-leg! The last time I saw him was at Jack

Nolans', the tavern-keeper at Fort Independence. He had come in to sell his skins, and spend his money on drink, as he did every three or four years, for he had no other way of spending it. Banks are few, and securities uncertain, among the Raphoes and Blackfeet! Peg drank more than he could pay for, and Nolans seized the old horse for the debt, and told its master to die when and where he pleased, but he would get neither liquor nor horse till he paid for both. Alas! there was no trapping at Fort Independence. Peg could as well have paid your national debt.

"The horse was accordingly locked up in an outhouse, the door being fastened with a huge padlock, the key of which hung as an ornament near Mr. Nolans' bed. Early in the morning, Peg rose, stepped a few paces back from the padlock, covered the lock with his rifle, blew it open, limped in, and in a trice was mounted on the old horse.

"Mr. Nolans, alarmed by the shot, had come out in his night-dress to see what was the matter, but only got a peep of Peg, with his leg projecting like a bowsprit between him and the sky, on the top of a prairie knoll, waving his hand as he and his old horse retired once more to live, and I suppose to die, among the Rocky Mountains!"

"What a life!" said I.

"Ah! my friend, you have never tried it! Once begun, it has a charm which acts like spirits to a confirmed drunkard; you may suffer from it, but habit prevents you from giving it up. I begin to fear I myself could never live in the settlements. As for such a man as Peg-leg Smith doing so, you might as well try and get an eagle to strut along the streets of New York."

The last time I saw the merchant was in Liverpool; and after a long chat, he wished to give me, as a parting gift—will the reader guess what?—a scalp of an Indian whom he had slain in battle!

I begged he might not take the trouble of searching for the relic. But a chord had been touched by the very mention of the scalp, and he fell into a reverie, staring at the fire while he slowly smoked his cigar. At last the puffs of smoke got quicker and quicker—the stern expression came to the eye—till, stamping with one foot on the floor, and clenching his hands, he said with intense energy—

"I shall yet do for him!"

"For whom?" I inquired.

"That scoundrel Raphoe Indian who shot my brother!"

In the rich and populous "settlement" of Liverpool he was dreaming of the Far West, and arranging, in his own mind, for his next attack upon the Raphoes, to revenge the death of a brother whom they had killed!

The last accounts I received of A. S., the merchant of the wilderness, were lately from an old friend who now resides in Mexico. On asking him whether he had ever heard of such a person, he replied, "His name has been well known in Mexico and the Far West for nearly thirty years as a very remarkable, honest, enterprising, and daring man. But I have lost sight of him for years. He returned, I believe, to Germany, after having made money in California, but could not resist the attractions of the wilderness, and so he went again back to the Far West.

"The last thing I heard about him," he continued, "was an incident very characteristic of the man. A diligence in which he was travelling near Mexico was attacked by a strong party of banditti, and robbed. The only one of the passengers who showed fight was a little, athletic, black-eyed man, who sat on his luggage with a loaded revolver in each hand, gazing with a stern look on the banditti.

"'I know,' he said, 'you cowardly scoundrels, that you can kill me and rob me, but not before two of you, at least, are first shot by me, for I never missed. So keep off!'

"They did keep off; and the merchant of the wilderness thus saved his life and property. I have not heard of him since."

Such a strange life of energy and courage is worth knowing about.

IN THE YO SEMITE VALLEY.

IN THE YO SEMITE VALLEY.

CHAPTER I.

FROM SAN FRANCISCO.

THE famous big trees of Talaveras county were my first object.

A steamer leaves San Francisco at four in the afternoon, and, after winding through the narrow and tortuous "sleughs" of the San Joaquin river, reaches Stockton in the early morning. Hence, a four-horse "Concord" coach leaves at six for Murphy's, where it arrives at about eight the same evening.

Let me describe a Concord coach.

First, it derives its name from the town in the eastern States where it is built, and is an overgrown loutish descendant of the English mail-coach of former days. It is usually painted bright red, and carries on its panels a glaring portrait either of a President, a maiden, or a general; over the door is written "U. S. Mail," generally translated "Uncle Sam's Mail;" and along the top are the names of the termini between which it runs.

Inside, are three seats, each made to hold three people: the back and front seats are of course the most comfortable, those who are on the middle bench having but a strap to lean against. Thus nine is the limit of inside accommodation; the limit outside has not yet been ascertained, but eight besides the driver may be comfortably seated, that is, if the word "comfort" is at all applicable to a Concord coach.

A most important part is its powerful break, applied by heavy pressure of the driver's right foot. These breaks are used in all American coaches and mud-waggons, and are indispensable in the steep country they traverse.

The luggage is strapped on to a vast platform behind; small parcels are put in the front boot, and miscellaneous light baggage is placed on the top. No springs would support this cumbrous body over Californian roads, so it is hung on stout leather thorough-braces.

The distance from Stockton to Murphy's is about eighty miles, travelled at an average speed of seven miles an hour. The road is good, for a new country, but little has as yet been done by art. It passes through grain-fields of from one to five thousand acres, the ground being absolutely level, and dotted with a sort of weeping oak. The last thirty miles of the road are through hilly country, lightly timbered with pine and flowering shrubs.

Murphy's is a pretty little country village in a mining

LEAVING THE PIER AT SAN FRANCISCO.

district, and boasts a good inn, owned by Mr. Perry, the proprietor of the Mammoth Grove. Its comforts are an agreeable surprise to the traveller, almost stifled as he is by the dust, which tries the temper and equanimity of the most amiable.

Mr. Perry runs a stage to the big trees—fifteen miles—every morning, returning to Murphy's in the evening. There is a good hotel at the Grove, situated under the very shadow of the trees; it is a great place of resort for a few weeks in the summer, as the country is famous for an abundance of game, and for the beauty of the surrounding scenery.

One of the largest trees, thirty-one feet in diameter, was felled some years ago, and a section of it sent to New York; its stump is roofed over, and is used as a floor for dancing upon.

The means taken for felling this tree were original and ingenious. A ring of bark was removed at a convenient height from the ground, and the trunk was bored through with augurs, each hole touching its neighbour; it was then overthrown by wedges driven in on one side, the whole operation lasting three weeks.

The immense size of the trees does not impress one at first: it takes some little time to realise their magnificent proportions. The tallest is about three hundred and thirty feet high, but not one appears to be symmetrically finished; all seem to have been broken off or severely injured by the fires which have from time to time swept through the forest.

As nearly three thousand rings can be counted on the stump of the tree above referred to, the largest are supposed to be nearly three thousand years old. The young trees are pretty, with light, graceful foliage.

The botanical name is *sequoia gigantea;* the Americans very justly objecting to its being called *Wellingtonia,* and retaliate on our impertinence by calling it *Washingtonia.* It is said that this tree is only indigenous in two other places, and both are in California, at the same altitude above the sea. Its bark grows in vertical ridges like buttresses, sometimes projecting as much as two feet, and a section of the tree shows where the solid wood has in some instances overgrown the bark, enclosing small patches of it. The fibre of the wood is like the California red-wood, soft and rather fine grained; it is light, the cubic foot weighing rather less than nineteen pounds.

Most of the largest trees have names on marble tablets affixed to their trunks, such as "The Mother of the Forest," "The Father of the Forest," "Florence Nightingale," "Richard Cobden," "Hercules," "The Pride of the Forest," &c.

The most beautiful and striking spot in California, some say in the world, is the Yo Semite Valley in Mariposa County, where are the highest known waterfalls. It is approached by stage from Stockton, through fine hill country affording some noble points of view, and intersected by many streams and rivers, of a muddy-red colour, owing to the operations of miners. The stage stops fifty-seven miles from the valley, at a small dull place called Coulterville, said to be 2,500 feet above the level of the sea.

On the 27th of June I started from Coulterville, in company with Mr. and Mrs. Baker, of Sacramento, who were so kind as to allow me to join their party.

We travelled on horseback, accompanied by a guide, and what few articles we required were strapped on to the saddles. Mrs. Baker possessed in an eminent degree the art of at once putting a stranger at his ease, and, like most American ladies, thoroughly understood the leading topics of the day, and how to express herself clearly and intelligibly. Such pleasant companions as Mr. and Mrs. Baker proved to be, materially added to the pleasure of the journey, and as we rode through the forests her clear sweet voice rang out the patriotic melodies the late rebellion has given birth to and cherished.

We left Coulterville at nine A.M., and after travelling up the hills all the forenoon along a dry waggon-road, soft with a reddish impalpable dust that found its way everywhere where it ought not, we reached the Bower Cave soon after noon. A few distant glimpses through the trees, as we ascended the mountains, showed the glorious snow-capped Sierra Nevadas to the east, and the hills, streams, valleys, and plains to the westward, through which we had already come.

This cave would not be much visited were it not on the road to the Yo Semite Valley, but it is rather a remarkable place. At any rate, it is very pleasant to leave the dry, dusty, hot, baking air of the upper earth, and descend a few steps to a cool and shady grotto.

INTERIOR OF CAVE.

At the bottom is a deep pool of clear green icy water, by the side of which grow a couple of trees whose top-

most branches are level with the ground above. A few stalactites hang from the roof, among which swallows and squirrels make their homes. I must add that the Frenchman and his wife who own the spot keep good cream, butter, and eggs, for the refreshment of the weary.

At half-past four in the afternoon we reached Black's, a wayside house eighteen miles from Coulterville, where travellers usually put up. Here we sat down to the best meal I tasted in California—plain meats and farm produce, but everything genuine and quite the best of its kind—so we made merry over our excellent fare. Then, rolling myself up in my Scotch plaid in the verandah, with my saddle-bags for a pillow, I fell asleep.

The next morning we started at half-past six along the mule trail which leads to the Valley, thirty-six miles distant.

Our way lay through much grander scenery, with views here and there over large tracts of country. The forest was never thick, but consisted chiefly of spruce and sugar pine, thinly growing in a red sandy soil, with granite or trap boulders cropping up. A group of these boulders was arranged in a hollow form like Stonehenge, enclosing an area about fifty feet in diameter, and a round boulder on the top of a slab seemed as if it must have been placed there by human hands.

The light underwood was composed principally of the manzanita, a celebrated mountain wood which takes a fine polish, but is seldom found to grow to any thickness, and can only be used in veneers. Although the best time for wild flowers had passed, there were many in bloom of rich and exquisite hues. As we reached the higher levels the species varied, and we saw quantities of sweet white azaleas.

ON THE HILL-TOP.

At last we topped the hill overlooking the valley, and a grand sight was before us. Its remarkable feature was that it appeared to be an enormous rent in the rocks, whose perpendicular sides had opened out. Its depth, and not the height of the hills surrounding it, was what struck us most. On their further sides the hills are not steep, while towards the valley they are almost perpendicular. It is over these that the water pours uninterruptedly from a great height, feeding the Yo Semite River, which is seen like a bright serpentine line along the bottom.

The descent occupied about an hour, and was tedious from its steepness and the roughness of the trail, and when we reached the foot we had still five miles to go to the hotel at the east end of the valley.

The trail lay through perfectly level park land, with long rich grass, and it abounded in picturesque retired spots, where nothing could be heard but the murmuring of the river and the distant thundering of the falls. As we looked up at the granite mountains, sheer rock faces of unequalled height and grandeur towering above our heads on either side, we began to realise what we had come so far to see. The melting snows threw their waters over the precipices at many points, but we saw only one of the grand falls, the Bridal Veil. In several places the river spreads out into a narrow still lake, and then again contracts to a rushing noisy stream.

One of the sights of the valley is the Mirror Lake. Here the mountains approach very closely on either side, and are perfectly reflected in a small sheet of glassy water. The effect is quite unique: one feels suspended in space—endless heights above, and boundless depths below; but this effect is only produced in the early morning, when the air is still and clear, and before the sun shines directly on the water.

IN THE YO SEMITE VALLEY.

CHAPTER II.

FROM THE VERNAL FALL.

THE two finest falls in the Valley, that is, those which contain the largest bodies of water, are on the same stream, the chief feeder of the Yo Semite River. For the latter part of the way they can only be approached on foot, over a rude trail through forest and among boulders.

The Vernal Fall is the one first reached, but its roaring appeals to the ear and its spray to the touch long before it is seen. It is only three hundred feet high, but is on the whole the most impressive, as the sheet of water is unbroken; while the Nevada Fall, although three times the height, strikes the side of the rock about half-way down, sending clouds of spray in all directions.

The rushing of such a volume of water produces a con-

THE VERNAL WATERFALL.

stant and unvarying wind, while the spray is scattered round for a long distance. Thus the soil is always moist, even during the hottest summers, and the trees and bushes are luxuriant, but all bow in one direction before the prevailing wind.

A very narrow trail made along the slippery face of a naked rock, leads from one waterfall to the other. The precipice over which the water pours has to be ascended by two long flights of ladders, the results of much perseverance and ingenuity; after which we come to the connecting quarter of a mile of smooth swift water. The ceaseless flow has worn the rocks away in circular basins, and the stream runs from one into another as if they were artificial.

The top of the Nevada Fall may be reached by laborious climbing, but it is beyond the route of most tourists, and there is little to reward one for the labour of the ascent. Precipitous rocks so lofty are probably to be found nowhere else in the world, and the effect is bewildering.

The Bridal Veil Fall is so called, because it breaks as soon as it tips over the rocks, and the water comes down in a sheet of spray like the most exquisite lace. Ever-changing tongues of foam course down its face, starting into existence, chasing one another, overtaking, uniting, vanishing; now swayed to one side, now to another, and now borne out by a breeze far from the rock, in a light cloud.

The Indians call it Pohono, the name of an evil spirit. Its height is upwards of nine hundred feet; but it contains the smallest body of water of any of the great falls, and dries up in the summer.

The Yo Semite Fall is the highest in the world, 2,548 feet; but it is caught by the rocks in two places, dividing it into three falls; the lower one is about 700 feet high, while the upper is about 1,448 feet, and between the two is a series of rapids rather than a fall.

I despair of being able to convey to the mind of a reader the emotions experienced at the sight of these stupendous falls. The enormous size both of them and of the mountains of rock is almost stupefying; the eye wanders up higher and higher, till the brain quite loses the power of judging heights and distances.

During last June, experiments were made by the Surveyor-General of California, Mr. Houghton, with the view of determining the volume of water pouring over the Yo Semite Fall. He selected a point below the Fall, where the stream is wide, and of nearly uniform depth, and where the current is comparatively slow.

He estimated the area of a section of the river at this point to be 77·83 square feet, and the quantity of water passing this point, 428,861 cubic feet per hour. But it must be observed that of the water pouring over the first and third falls, a large amount is converted into spray, and the evaporation is very great; also that the river runs over a loose sandy and gravelly soil, from the foot of the last fall to the point of the above measurements, and that much must be lost by percolation.

From these causes it is estimated that from the first

dash over the upper fall to the point of measurement the volume is diminished at least twenty per cent., which would give a total volume at the first-named point of over a half a million cubic feet per hour.

A ROADSIDE STREAM.

Taking the stage, I passed through Sonora, San Andreas, Mokelumne Hill, Jackson, and Drytown, and reached the Latrobe railway station on the morning of the 5th of July, where I joined the direct overland route between San Francisco and New York.

Leaving Latrobe by the evening train, we arrived at Shingle Springs after a couple of hours' run. This place, to the eastward of the 121st degree of longitude, is at present the end of that railroad which, starting from Sacramento, is some day to cross the continent.

Gigantic as the task appears, it is steadily and perseveringly pursued: year after year do trains run further and further to the eastward, and the railway levels mount higher and higher. The Sierra Nevada mountains once crossed, the road will advance much faster; and I am persuaded that the central plains of this great continent will be crossed by steam before many years are over.

Leaving Shingle Springs by a six-horse stage, I arrived at Placerville at eleven P.M. The next morning, at half-past four, I rose to go on by the early coach. When it arrived I found that it was full, two gentlemen having engaged six seats, that they might sleep at ease. The night being now so far spent, I asked one of them to rent me a seat; but he replied that the pleasure of obliging me on his arrival at Placerville was not the motive that had induced him to engage his three seats at San Francisco. I begged him not to let it prey upon his mind; and I really don't think he did, as I saw him settle comfortably down into his feather pillows for another nap as the stage drove off. I tried to look happy, cheerful, contented, &c.; how far I succeeded, history must decide.

However, when the second coach arrived in the afternoon, I found a vacant seat, and pursued my journey to Virginia City.

The road between that place and Shingle Springs is always kept in first-rate order; during the summer it is watered every night, and so kept hard. The coaches are first-class, the six horses are always carefully chosen and well matched, and the drivers are selected for their skill and good character.

It is said that some of the "tallest" driving in the States may be seen on this road, and, as far as my experience goes, I certainly never saw such driving. One passes heavy waggons drawn by long teams, both journeying east and west; the road is often narrow and steep, with sharp turns; and when the driver, rapidly swinging his six horses round a bluff, sometimes comes suddenly on a waggon labouring up the hill, only great skill and experience, and firm nerve, prevent either a collision on the one hand, or a capsize on the other.

The hills are descended at full gallop, and ascended at a smart trot. At one place it became necessary for us to go very near the edge of the steep; the earth crumbled and sunk under the outer wheels, and for a moment the coach heeled over a little, but, at the pace we were going, soon recovered itself. Accidents are very rare.

BY COACH OVER THE SIERRA NEVADAS.

BY COACH OVER THE SIERRA NEVADAS.

FROM PLACERVILLE TO VIRGINIA CITY.

IN crossing the Sierra Nevadas there are two high points, the First and Second Summits, said to be about six thousand feet above the level of the sea.

Between these lies Lake Tahoe, a large sheet of fresh water about forty miles in diameter.

We passed the First Summit in the evening, just before sundown, and the view was magnificent; mountain after mountain rolling away in the distance as far as the eye could reach. I have seen many of the celebrated views of the world, but never one which seemed to command so vast and immeasurable a view of this round earth.

From the First Summit, the American river flows to the westward. During our ascent we followed its banks for many miles, and saw in several places the old emigrant road used in former days before the present one was made.

Anything less like a road, or more like the track of an avalanche, could scarcely be imagined; and one could in some degree conceive what were the obstacles surmounted by the hardy, gallant pioneers of the far far West. In a few short years, Yankee go-aheaditiveness will have wiped out even these memorials of the past.

The western slope of the Sierra Nevadas abounds with quail of two species. Near the plains is the common California quail, but higher up is the mountain quail, distinguished by a crest of two long feathers, which quiver with every quick, nervous motion of its little head, as it runs over the rocks and among the bushes. Both species are numerous, of beautiful plumage, and good eating. They are difficult to catch alive, but I have seen a large cageful of them at a wayside house among the mountains.

Descending at a break-neck pace from the First Summit, we reached the borders of Lake Tahoe, whose southern shores we followed for nearly twenty miles. It was now night, but a full moon gave to the scene a peculiar beauty, lighting up points of the most distant hills, and shadowing valleys in the deepest gloom.

All day had I been jolted on the top of the coach, but when night came I took my place inside, where was a vacant seat.

This was my first experience of a night spent in a Con-

MOUNTAIN SCENERY.

cord coach. Looking back to my first middle-watch as a midshipman, to my last middle-watch as a lieutenant, or to my first night after I caught the measles, I can remember no night of horror equal to my first night's travel on the Overland Route.

An American friend, who had himself crossed the plains, had recommended me to bring an air-pillow. This became my mainstay: I sat on it by day, or interposed it between the hard side of the coach and my ragged skin and jaded bones, and by night I put my head through the hole in the middle and wore it as a collar, like a degraded Chinaman. This saved the sides of my head during my endeavours to sleep, but occasionally a heavier jolt than usual would strike my head violently against the roof, driving it down between my shoulders.

I remember nothing between the shores of Lake Tahoe and the Second Summit; here I certainly did look out of the window, and then fell to bumping about again until we stopped for a short time at Carson City, at one A.M.

Here we got out and stamped around for a few minutes, while the horses were being changed, and were amused by a lady who had no money wherewith to pay her fare any farther, and at the same time declined to alight. The mail agent was in an awkward fix: he did not like to engage in a fray in the dead hours of the night, as the awakened neighbours would be sure to side with the woman they did not know, for the pleasure of abusing the man they did know; and yet if he allowed her to proceed, the amount of her fare would be charged against his pay. At last, however, he was persuaded to leave her in possession by her assurance that she was a person of great consideration, owning houses and lands in Virginia City, and that everybody knew where she lived. So I poked my head into my air-pillow again, and off we went.

At four A.M., just as the day was breaking, we stopped at the door of the International Hotel, Virginia City, and, more dead than alive, I fell asleep on a real bed for several hours.

A very frowsy-looking saint, bound for the Great Salt Lake, came with us, and started for his Eden two hours after arrival.

Virginia City is a remarkable specimen of the towns that seem to spring up by magic in the mining districts. It is situated near the foot of a conspicuous hill, Mount Davidson, in a land where rain never falls, where not a blade of grass is visible, and where trees are only to be seen in one distant valley. It lies in the focus of the rays of the sun reflected from the naked hills, a dry and uninviting evidence of underground wealth.

All that part of the State of Nevada, recently admitted into the Union, is known as the Washoe country, and is celebrated for the richness of its silver mines. The rain-bearing clouds that come floating in from the Pacific Ocean are caught by the Sierra Nevada Mountains, and fall condensed before they reach the Washoe country.

Snow falls heavily in winter on the Sierra Nevadas,

FROM PLACERVILLE TO VIRGINIA CITY.   261

and on the high plateau of Nevada State, which is much more elevated than California. These snows melting in summer, feed two or three considerable streams, which flow

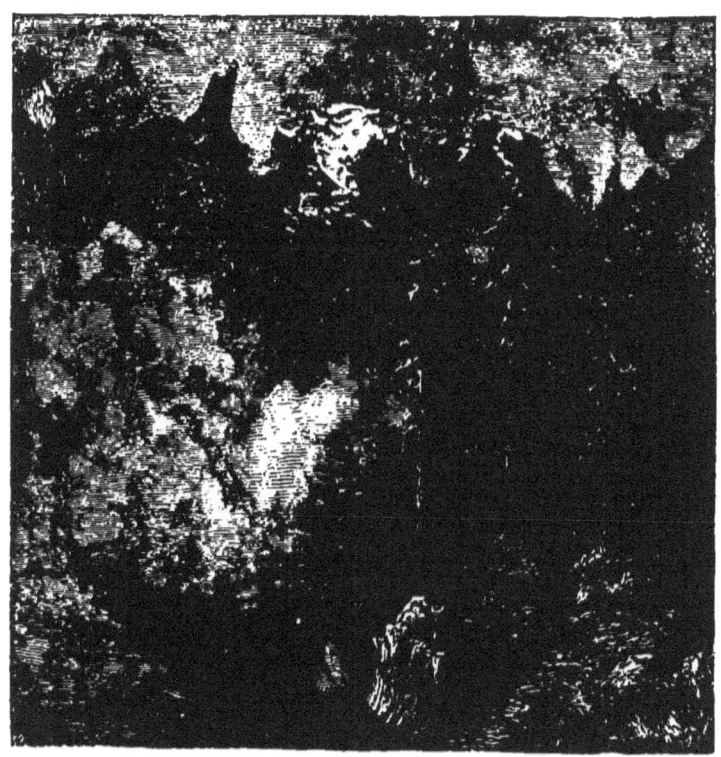

RAIN-BEARING CLOUDS IN THE SIERRA.

for some distance and are then lost in sinks in valleys, where a few cotton-trees grow.

The ground is hard, and mostly covered with a sage-brush like the common garden-sage. A few attempts at irrigation have succeeded, and in one or two places round the town are small vegetable gardens.

There are many well-built brick buildings in Virginia City, including two theatres. The mines gave birth to three towns, Gold Hill, Silver City, and Virginia City; and houses have now sprung up between them, making one continuous street, three or four miles long, running along the side of a hill, which is burrowed and tunnelled in every direction.

Like most speculative towns, Virginia City lives in a condition of normal collapse; every man you meet assures you that the place is "caving in," and that the mines are "played out;" yet, if you walk round the town, you will see houses springing up, and much business being transacted in the "stores."

Beautiful specimens of petrified wood are found in the neighbourhood. They are very remarkable, as there are now no trees within miles of the spot; and they seem to show that this country was once well wooded, and enjoyed a totally different climate.

About five miles from Virginia City are some hot springs. I had not time to visit them, but I believe that there are several acres covered with small geysers of various temperatures.

Some letters I had brought with me, assisted by kind recommendations from Mr. Rising, secured for me the privilege of visiting the Gould and Curry silver mine, in company with the foreman.

To the uninitiated, I do not know that there is any great interest in a mine. One mine is generally very much like another. One is sometimes dirtier than another; in one there is sometimes more bad air than in another; in one there is sometimes more black

A SMALL GEYSER.

water than in another; but there is a strong family likeness.

The Gould and Curry mine formed no exception. We entered the side of the hill, following a level tunnel, and carrying greasy candles; we went down shafts, clambered up ladders, crawled along drains, examined muddy pieces of rock, tapped them with pickaxes, broke off lumps and held them to the candles, and declared they were very beautiful and very rich. We were soon wet through with perspiration, and envied the miners in the scantiest possible clothing.

Although quite tired out after a couple of hours, I had still to follow the foreman on his rounds, and did not reach the upper earth till I had spent three hours and a half in this noisome hole.

But although such a long visit was not very entertaining to me, two or three Californian gentlemen made up the party, and I was able to learn something from their remarks.

The Gould and Curry silver mine is one of the richest, and probably the best worked, in the world. The Company does everything on a handsome scale: it gives the resident manager £2,500 a-year, and a good house; most of its buildings and workshops are of brick and hewn stone; and no expense is spared in order that the works should be conducted as well as possible. The silver is contained in quartz, which is crushed in a steam quartz-crushing machine, worked with ninety stampers; and it is found to contain twenty-five per cent. of gold.

Many mines are worked in the neighbourhood, but none afford returns so rich as the Gould and Curry. It has a great advantage in being on a hill, because the quartz is brought out in waggons, which run down on a railroad by their own impetus to the storerooms and mills below.

A visit to the top of Mount Davidson, which overhangs the town, rewards one with an extensive view of the country. The ascent is steep and stony, but the sight from the top is one never to be forgotten.

MOUNT DAVIDSON.

The clearness of the sky in that pure mountain air makes the view almost illimitable, but it is only the great distance one is able to see, and the endless succession of mountain ranges, that is beautiful; for owing to the absence of all verdure, the nearer country looks painfully barren and repulsive. The grey sage-brush, which everywhere covers the ground, has a dreary, monotonous appearance, that is wearisome both to eye and heart. At the top is a flagstaff, seventy feet long, whence usually wave the stars and stripes, but from the town below it looks like a stick with a handkerchief on the end of it. I believe Virginia City is about the ninth or tenth highest in the world.

But to resume the journey. At half-past six in the morning of the 10th of July, I left Virginia in a Concord coach. At last I felt myself fairly off on the great Overland Route, and a very charming journey it promised to be.

The morning was cool, the sun was rising over the hills, and there was no wind to make the dust unendurable.

Our coach was nearly a new one, and six beautiful glossy black horses, with flowing manes and tails, proudly champed their bits and pawed the ground, as we waited at the door of the stage-office for our final orders. Presently we dashed down the hill, through the lower streets of the town, and were soon rattling over the plain through the eternal sage-brush.

The coach was quite full, nine inside and one out, the greatest number ever carried on this road. Three Mexican women and an American lady were among the passengers; the other five were miners, and proprietors of mule or waggon trains.

SUCCESSION OF MOUNTAIN RANGES.

But of the "charming" prospect every mile of the overland journey more completely disenchanted us. We had not gone far before we began to feel cramped; then the heat of the sun made us hot and irritable; and not only was there a difficulty about stowing away one's feet, but we had even to fit-in our knees, one with another, and then occasionally give and take pretty smart blows, caused by the jostling of the carriage; and finally, most of the men chewed tobacco, and those who occupied centre seats had to exert considerable skill to spit clear of the other passengers.

Americans are generally adepts in this art, but we had one or two unskilful professors, although it must be admitted that they had hardly a fair opportunity of showing off their proficiency, from the jolting of the coach. Occasionally they would unconcernedly expectorate among the baggage on the floor. The smell caused by this abominable practice was intolerable and sickening at first, until one became somewhat accustomed to it.

In railway carriages, in the best hotels, and even at the renowned West Point military academy, the disgusting habit of chewing tobacco prevails.

Pocket handkerchiefs do not appear to be common, and my fellow-passengers occasionally resorted to the primitive custom probably handed down to us from the patriarchal ages, and religiously preserved among the London arabs.

The females of the party had many small packages which they insisted on having inside with them. In this department the ladies from Mexico were distinguished; one basket, with the contents of which I must confess they were truly hospitable, quite disarming the grumblers. It contained cheese, biscuits, dried fish, and onions.

After we had been an hour or two on the road the heat became still more oppressive; a light westerly breeze carried the dust along with us, which was at times stifling. The severe discomforts of this travelling can hardly be exaggerated, but one learns to endure them.

The character, the language, and the manners of the class of people who chiefly use this route, however, became if possible even more repugnant to me each day. These I could not endure without disgust, and at the end of my journey, in spite of all attempts at reserve or civility, I felt myself cowed and humiliated in a manner not to be described. Even now I cannot think of my companions in some parts of the overland journey without a shudder.

We changed horses about every ten miles, and soon discovered that distance did not lend enchantment to the horses. The beautiful long-tailed prancers of the morning were shortly changed for muddy, bony beasts, with drumlike skins, which suggested the idea that they were only walking about to save funeral expenses.

But the most complete disenchantment of the charming promise with which we started the journey was still in reserve. After bolting our dinners at Cottonwood, forty-five miles from Virginia City, we found that the coach went no further, and that our journey must be pursued in mud-waggons.

HUT ON THE SIERRA.

I must endeavour to give some idea of a mud-waggon. If it had springs, it would be something like what in

England is called a spring van; but it hasn't. Like a Concord coach, it rides on thorough-braces; its sides and top are of leather, or folds of stout painted canvas, stretched over a wooden frame; inside' are three seats, each carrying three persons; a platform behind carries the mail-bags and heavier luggage, while the front boot holds the express bags and small parcels; and there is one seat for a passenger alongside the driver. These carriages are generally painted red, without expensive or elaborate ornament, and drawn by four, or sometimes six horses.

Some mud-waggons are rather better than others, but all are very rough. It may be doubted, however, whether any better kind of carriage would stand the hard usage they receive.

Some of the teams are fierce little mustangs, which draw very well, but are difficult to drive; others are respectable old carriage-horses that have seen better days; but staging is severe work, and soon kills them. I did see one fine horse that had been staging for ten years in the wildest country, and appeared ready for ten years more, but he was an exceptionally sturdy old fellow.

The stages profess to stop for three meals a day, and to allow half an hour each time. Between Virginia City and Salt Lake City the number of passengers and the hour at which they may be expected is telegraphed from station to station.

Ten minutes after arrival the food is on the table; ten minutes afterwards, you choke yourself as the driver calls out, "All aboard;" and ten minutes after that again, you are fairly under weigh, inhaling dust; and ten minutes later still you are suffering from a severe attack of indigestion.

During the first part of the journey, tolerably punctual time is kept, but time once lost cannot be made good afterwards, and as the home stations are at irregular distances, the results are apt to be inconvenient.

One night at eleven o'clock we reached a home station where we ought, according to the way-bill, to have breakfasted. Breakfast was ready, but, dead tired as we were, we refused to turn out.

The driver warned us we were a long way from the next home station; but who thinks of the morrow when he is worn out with fatigue? The next day we had to pay for our neglect, as we did not reach a home station until two in the afternoon. By that time we were all more or less ill, and only a box of prunes from my hamper kept us at all alive.

The journey from Virginia City to Salt Lake City lasted five days and four nights.

On the evening of the second day we crossed a brook called Reoso River, and passed through a small town called Austin City. This was the only place on the road worthy of the name of a town, and it contained a few brick and stone houses. It stands among the hills, and is purely a mining town, some of the mines opening on to its street.

The road lay through desert alkali plains, barren red

hills and mountains, marshes, and sands. The winds traversing these plains become impregnated with the

A LEVEL MOUNTAIN PASS.

alkali, which causes a bad taste in the mouth, and dries up the lips and the skin on the face and hands.

In some places there were pretty views: some of the hill tops and a view of the valleys were relieved by pine and cedar scrub, but little can be said in favour of the scenery. The ground was invariably covered with dull grey sage-brush; the ranges of hills and mountains run north and south, and between them are absolutely level plains, varying from ten to twenty miles in breadth. The hills are seldom ascended, as in almost every instance there is a natural pass through them on nearly the same level as the plains. One of these, nearly four miles long, had the regularity of a railroad cutting.

It was in these passes that two or three years ago the Indians used to attack the stage.

SALT LAKE CITY.

SALT LAKE CITY.

THE CITY AND ITS PEOPLE.

AT a distance of twenty-five miles from Salt Lake City we forded the River Jordan, the water being about four feet deep. It runs in a northerly direction about forty miles, from the fresh-water Utah Lake to the Great Salt Lake.

These lakes lie at each end of a valley some fifteen miles in breadth. At the north end, and on an elevated "bench," is situated the famous city of the Latter Day Saints, bearing the appearance of white specks on a green ground—a striking contrast to the surrounding arid desert.

On our right rose grand mountains, six or seven thousand feet high, thrown like a sheltering arm behind the City of the Saints; and on our left stretched the broad Salt Lake, with two mountainous islands standing out in bold relief, while the River Jordan, passing almost under our feet, was seen winding its way to the Dead Sea.

The air of these regions is so pure, that distant objects are seen with a distinctness very deceiving.

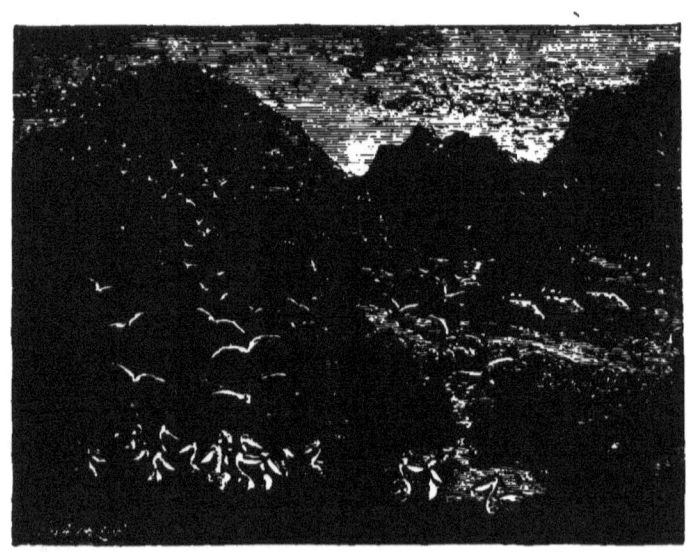

BANKS OF UTAH LAKE.

The drive into the city passes between fields irrigated by streams descending from the eastern hills. We changed horses every ten miles, and as we advanced, signs of prosperity were more numerous, for we saw houses, gardens, and small farms.

At length it became dark, and it was not until 9.30

P.M. that our long long drive terminated as we drew up in front of the Salt Lake House.

I was too much knocked up for sight-seeing on the first day after my arrival. Without feeling actually tired, I found myself continually dropping off to sleep; but the excitement of the journey gradually wore off.

BANKS OF UTAH LAKE.

The first piece of news we heard by telegraph that morning was that a stage-coach, which runs three times a-week between Virginia City in the Idahoe territory and Salt Lake City, had been attacked and robbed by highwaymen. The driver and four passengers out of five were shot dead; the fifth fell down severely wounded in the bottom of the coach, and was only saved by the bodies of his companions falling on him. The murderers escaped with a booty of seventy thousand dollars, or fourteen thousand pounds, in gold dust.

Last summer this same stage was robbed, and the passengers murdered; some of the robbers were caught and hanged, while others escaped.

The general impression given by Salt Lake City is an agreeable one.

The streets divide the town into ten-acre blocks: they are all a hundred and twenty-eight feet broad, and at right angles to each other. On each side is a stream of living water, and rows of cotton-wood and locust-trees border the side walks.

There is but one main street, in which the houses are built close to each other; everywhere else each house stands in its own garden or orchard. Some of them are large, two or three stories high, built of burnt bricks, red sandstone, or granite, but most are of white sun-dried bricks. They look clean and cheerful: the door-posts, window-sills, &c., are of wood, painted bright green, or of rich red sandstone, and creepers adorn the walls.

The gardens are well and tastefully kept, and fruit-trees are particularly successful. The streets chiefly used are gravelled; and as the plateau on which the town stands slopes gently to the southward, there is good drainage.

Altogether, few towns have been so judiciously designed and so perfectly built; few enjoy so great natural advantages, which have been cleverly made the

A STREET IN SALT LAKE CITY.

most of. The barren country we passed through would have prepared us to appreciate any place where there might be a spare blade of grass, but Salt Lake City would be considered beautiful anywhere.

The city is four thousand feet above the level of the sea, so the climate has greater extremes than that of England. In summer it is hot and dry, and rain rarely falls at any season; in winter there are heavy snows, which caused great suffering to the Mormons on their first arrival.

On the morning of Sunday, July 9th, I attended divine service in the rooms of a Young Men's Literary Association lately formed. It was conducted by a Congregationalist clergyman, a Scotchman, the Rev. Norman M'Leod, Chaplain to the Forces stationed here. He is a gallant, determined fellow, of considerable force of character.

In the afternoon I attended the Mormon service, prepared to hear something of Mormon doctrines, or perhaps some gospel truths with which I could myself agree, but was utterly disappointed.

The people were assembled in a large booth in the Temple Block. It is one of the squares, which has been walled in, and on which the temple is being built.

An address was given by a cadaverous-looking man. He urged the great weight his opinion of Mormonism ought to have with his audience, because, he said, he had tried all other religions and found them to be false. He said he was educated as a Baptist, but that religion did not satisfy him: he felt he wanted more, so he tried Presbyterianism; but that did not satisfy him, so he tried the Church of England and various sects, till at last he had found a home among the Mormons, and was happy. This climax was received with a sensation approximating to applause.

After the service, we strolled round the Temple Block, which, like the other squares or blocks in the city, is ten acres in extent. Besides the booth in which the service was held, it contained two finished and two unfinished buildings. The former are the tabernacle and the endowment house.

The tabernacle is a long building, like a chapel, with a round roof; the sun's rays, emblems of divinity, being carved in wood at the ends. I did not go inside. The interior of the endowment house can of course only be seen by saints; but from without it appears to be a plain two-storied house.

The new tabernacle is to be an oval building, surmounted by a huge dome, sustained on oblong red sandstone buttresses, in place of walls. The spaces between the pillars are to serve for windows and doors, and to be filled in winter by large glass frames on rollers. It is intended to hold fifteen thousand people.

It is hard and thankless to condemn a whole people, but the more I saw of the Mormons, the more was I convinced of the utter corruption of their chief men, and of the blind folly of the lower class. I believe Mormonism may be described as a system of extravagant fanaticism and unbounded licentiousness.

At the north end of the town are some hot sulphur

springs. The waters are much resorted to, and are considered very healthy.

Great attention has been paid to the internal economy of the city. It is divided into twenty wards, each of which is presided over by its own bishop, and controlled by its own sanitary and other officers, who all report regularly to Brigham Young.

Among these officers are the water-masters, whose duty it is to see that the water of the streams is fairly divided among the streets by day and among the gardens by night. These last depend for their moisture entirely upon irrigation, but when carefully tended they are very fruitful. All English fruits and vegetables thrive well; the currant grows to a great size, but its skin becomes hard, and it loses its flavour.

Ice is stored in the winter in large quantities, and is cheap even through the dry hot summer.

At Salt Lake City I made the acquaintance of Captain Charles Dahlgren, son of the distinguished American Admiral. He took me to Camp Douglas, where the American troops were stationed. A cheerful site has been chosen for their barracks on a plateau somewhat higher than the town, and distant from it about two miles to the eastward.

Three newspapers are published at Salt Lake—two in the city, and one, the *Vidette*, in the Camp. This last is a Gentile daily paper, and is probably safer in the Camp than it would be in the city. The *Deseret News* is a weekly Mormon paper, printed and published at the

Tithing Office; and there is also a daily Mormon paper.

At only one shop in Mormondom could books be purchased, and they were few in number and of the most paltry description. This is a significant fact with regard to a town which has a population of at least ten thousand souls.

It is difficult to estimate the amount of personal safety in the city, but there is no doubt that there is a most perfect system of espionage, and that little goes on with which the Prophet of the Lord—as Brigham Young is styled—is not made acquainted.

An artisan told me that seventeen years ago he joined the Mormons, and left them again about two years since. He said he still had some faith in Mormonism as it first existed, when there was probably a good deal of earnest piety among them. He held that now it was entirely changed and corrupted, and that the chiefs were a set of the lowest, most sensual, and degraded men.

I doubt whether half-a-dozen years ago life was safe for any one offending Brigham Young, but now, in the presence of the troops, the Mormon authorities would be afraid to have a man made away with. Yet some years ago a band of men existed, called Danites, or the destroying angels, whose business it was to execute the vengeance of the Prophet. They are now, however, released from that duty. One of them was pointed out to me, a man of most ferocious appearance; he was drunk, and driving a waggon through the street.

The town, however, has generally a sober and moral aspect; no retail liquor shops are allowed, and it is rare to see a drunken man. Offences are few. Sunday is scrupulously respected, and the people walk about in an orderly and quiet manner in their "Sabbath-day suits."

I was warned by Gentile residents not to send my letters through the post, and was positively assured that they are often opened, and, if considered expedient, burned.

As a people the Mormons are supercilious and insolent to outsiders, generally treating them with coldness and reserve—often with rudeness. There is great jealousy against them, and no prudent effort is spared to render their residence here uncomfortable. The insulting bearing of the Mormon hotel keeper of the Salt Lake House, his indifference to the comfort of his guests, the bad food and slovenliness of the establishment, made me rejoice when on Sunday night I moved into a boarding-house, kept by Mrs. King, where I spent the remainder of my stay in the enjoyment of cleanliness and civility.

The Mormon leaders are evidently in tribulation respecting the fate of their sect. The Speaker of the House of Congress, and other influential Americans who have lately visited Salt Lake City, plainly said that the Federal Government would insist on its laws being respected.

During the late rebellion, the Mormons cannot be accused of having assisted either party, In the most candid, unblushing way they gloried in the strife between

North and South, and prophesied the disruption of the Union. Of course, they looked forward to asserting their own independence—a future they keep steadily in view; and the complete triumph of the North has been a serious disappointment to them. Some of the sermons preached during the rebellion were little else than treason and sedition.

Seven-tenths of the population are from the British Isles, the remainder being Swedes, Danes, Norwegians, or Americans. The leading men are generally 'cute Yankees, while the others are from the most ignorant classes of various countries, especially remote parts of Wales and Scotland. It is a disgrace to England that this should be so.

It is argued that as polygamy and murder are essential parts of Mormonism, a Mormon missionary is in fact soliciting people to commit a crime, and may therefore be apprehended and bound over to be of good behaviour. I say murder, because every Mormon, on donning his endowment robes, swears that, if directed to do so, he is prepared to take the life of a brother who violates his oaths or speaks against the Mormon priesthood. In Prussia the former view of the case is taken, so there are no missionaries there. When we remember that from the shores of Old England hundreds of poor deluded creatures annually cross the sea and the desert, and arrive at Salt Lake City, it would be well if some steps could be taken to stop the proselytizing of the missionaries. Whatever modicum of good or of genuine piety there may have been among the early Mormons, their city is now a hotbed of vice, ignorance, and sensuality.

Brigham Young gives one the idea of a man of strong character and determined will. He is about sixty years of age, but looks ten years younger. His manner is perfectly natural, without the smallest vanity or arrogance, and he seemed by far the most superior Mormon I saw.

Yet vanity or affectation might well be expected in a man who has done what he has done.

It is not easy to realise what noble qualities must have been essential to the man who led a small body of people into the most desolate and least-known part of the New World; who cheered and encouraged them during days of great hardship; and, after seventeen years, has built up in this distant valley a well-ordered town, surrounded with smiling farms and suburbs. However much the Mormons may now be degraded and deluded, their leader must have been no common man to have performed his life's work.

From many things I heard, I am somewhat inclined to fear that, in spite of his talents and some admirable qualities, he is at heart a bad and wicked man; but no one will blame me if I shrink from too hasty a judgment.

I requested permission to visit the schools, and Brigham Young directed Mr. Campbell, the superintendent of education, to take me round. There were, however, only two in session at the time, and of these two I formed but a poor opinion, both from the appearance of the children and from their stock of knowledge.

Four of us Gentiles hired a carriage-and-pair, and drove across the valley—twenty miles—to visit a point on the Great Salt Lake, where is a small inn, and where boats are kept.

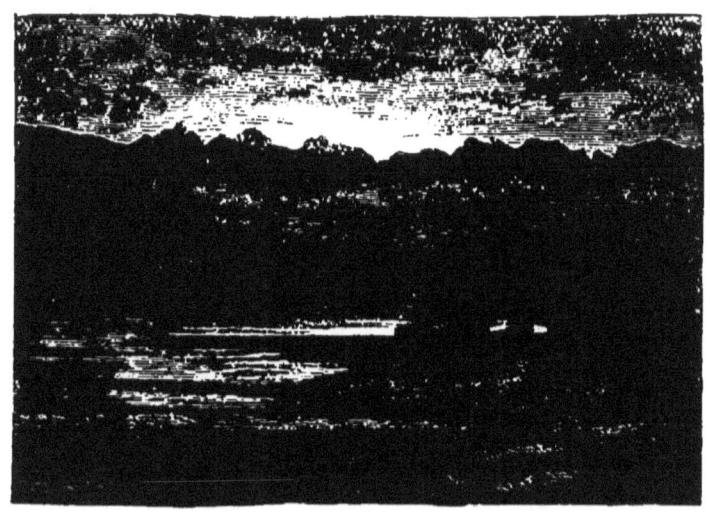

SALT LAKE AT SUNSET.

The shores of the lake are covered with dark brown salt to a depth of three or four inches, and the only living creatures we could detect were minute flies, myriads of which settled on the water in patches, looking like scum until, on being touched, they rose in a cloud.

The water holds in solution the greatest possible quantity of salt. It is of a deep blue—an effect probably caused by the salt, which makes it so dense as materially to check a boat sailing through it, though making her float lightly.

When we bathed, we found it very buoyant; and when we dived, its great specific gravity forced it into our eyes, noses, and ears to an extent that was acutely painful. One of our party courageously dived with the view of reaching the bottom, and when he came up his sufferings were so severe that we were quite alarmed lest he should be seriously injured: however, patience and a little fresh water at length relieved us, leaving us sadder and wiser men.

BY COACH THROUGH INDIAN RAIDS.

BY COACH THROUGH INDIAN RAIDS.

SALT LAKE TO ATCHISON.

ACCOUNTS of the eastern road were gloomy: rumours of Indian troubles, of drivers and travellers murdered, and stage-horses driven off, were not wanting when I left the Salt Lake for a journey of about twelve hundred miles to Atchison, on the Missouri. Our "mud-waggon" was a poor makeshift, and our horses were but sorry beasts.

As the stage professed to start at four A.M., I rose at three, and came down-stairs at the half-hour, to "fix a bite" before starting. At that moment the waggon drove up, and the driver declared it was four o'clock, and he could not wait a moment. I bundled in my chattels, and we drove off. Presently we stopped at a house in the suburbs, to pick up another passenger. The driver, with many execrations, surlily declared he was behind time, and could not wait a moment.

This passenger, who had not finished his breakfast, understood the language which had been lost on me, and produced a bottle and glass, which the driver enjoyed,

ROCKS IN ECHO CAÑON.

while the passenger concluded his meal at his leisure. Presently he got up on the box-seat, which had been refused me, and we went on our way.

I have no doubt that a box of cigars and a keg of

whisky judiciously applied would have smoothed at least some of the unpleasantness of stage-travel.

After ascending mountains the whole forenoon, we came to a plateau of comparatively good land, watered by the Weber and Bear Rivers. These are separated from each other by a rocky ridge, which we passed through by a gorge called Echo Cañon.

The forms assumed here by the soft red sandstone were more grotesque and striking than on any other part of the road. In some places we saw solid buttresses projecting far from the side of the rock, or standing out like towers, unconnected with the cliff, and in other places were caverns and archways, with the face of the rock seamed in all directions.

During the first two days we passed upwards of a hundred west-going waggons. It must be a hard road for emigrants; but men, women, and children all appeared the very picture of health. The cattle were usually poor, and in some places the road was literally lined with the bones of beasts who had died from cold, starvation, drought, or overwork. These long trains of waggons were sources of frequent pleasure.

Sometimes we were detained for a short time in the neighbourhood of an encampment, where the waggons were "coralled," the camp fires lighted, the cooking-stoves at work, the jaded cattle in the distance trying to pick up a meal, and little heaps of children rolling over each other in the dust. In these cases we always found the emigrants cheerful, in good spirits, and anxious to be sociable. When their party happened to include an aged or sick person, their thoughtfulness and care for his comfort was quite touching.

A horseshoe bend of a river is often chosen as a camping-ground, because the coralle of waggons is placed on the narrow neck, while the cattle graze on the broad enclosed land, and are easily caught when wanted. These

A MORMON CARAVAN.

emigrant trains have on several occasions been attacked by Indians, both when coralled and while on the road, but in no case with success.

It is estimated that about five thousand waggons, with an average of four souls each, cross these plains every year. This annual emigration of twenty thousand persons is a constant drain that no country but America could sustain without feeling it a serious loss. It is, besides, an evidence of the boundless resources of the United States, which are ever developing more and more, to an extent of which few people in the Old World have any idea.

For the first three days I was the only passenger, and having the interior of the waggon to myself, succeeded

A MORMON CARAVAN.

by crafty disposal of my blankets and kit in making myself tolerably comfortable. Sometimes on arrival at a station we found no mules, and had to rest and feed our team and take them on another stage.

On each side of the road were here and there burrows of ground squirrels and prairie dogs. The latter is a comical animal, not the least like a dog: he is a sort of ground rat, or rather like a grey guinea-pig. When the coach is heard he comes up to see it go by, and squats himself on the brink of his hole, where he gives vent to a peculiar squeak, which people have thought fit to designate a bark.

These prairie dogs congregate in villages, and make a great noise as each sits at his front door; but the least offensive movement on the part of the passer-by, the lifting of a stick or the presenting of a gun, sends them all out of sight in an instant.

A sort of large grouse is also seen, called by some the sage-hen, and by others the prairie chicken; it differs from the grouse in the legs not being feathered.

On the evening of the second day we came to a river known as the North Fork. The night was dar', and in fording it we went a few yards out of the way and stuck in the mud. The driver had an assistant with him who held the reins and beat the mules with a rope, while the former jumped into the water, broke his whip over them, dragged them from one side to the other, and lavished upon them all the most endearing epithets from the slang dictionary of a Western rowdy.

Strange to say, even this had no effect; all four mules quietly lay down, with their heads just above the stream, and broke the pole. There was no help for it but to unhitch the team, which the two drivers drove to the bank, leaving me in the waggon with the water up to the floor. I cried to them to carry me on shore, which after a little hesitation one of them did. We walked to the nearest station, about half a mile off, where we slept.

In the morning I was the first up, so I lighted the fire, and began preparing breakfast. Soon the drivers joined me, and one of them addressed me thus:—

"I guess, Mister, you've travelled round a bit."

I replied that I had "travelled some," and inquired what made him think so.

He said, "Wall, now! when we was stuck in the crick last night you sat still and says nothin'; now if you'd a begun cussin at us, as some does, there you might have stayed, or got yourself wet walking out."

After this we became bosom friends of course, and he borrowed my knife, which he quite forgot to return until he had been asked for it three times. He asked me many minute details about my personal and family history, and expressed great admiration for the cat-o'-nine-tails, which he said was just the "institootion" the American army wanted.

We persuaded some emigrants to lend us a team of eight oxen, which dragged the coach out at once, after which we spliced the pole and pursued our journey.

On the morning of the fifth day, I overtook Mr. Reynolds, the superintendent of the telegraph line, and travelled with him as far as Denver City. It was to me a matter of no small satisfaction that he consented to allow me to go with him, and a favour of which I am very sensible. I was fortified with letters from Colonel George to the officers commanding the troops along the road, and these, together with Mr. Reynolds' office, which he made the most of, secured us attentions by the way, large escorts, and occasionally government mules.

At first our escort numbered only four men, but as we penetrated to the more dangerous country, it was increased to twelve. We were ourselves well armed with rifles and revolvers. The escort was changed every ten or fifteen miles, when we came to small detachments posted at those intervals.

Generally I found one of the escort very glad to travel in the waggon, and to allow me to ride his horse—a benefit to both parties.

The stage has been molested by Indians on more than one occasion. It was attacked a fortnight before I passed, by about seventy. There were seven or eight passengers, who, with the escort, made up twenty persons, and after an hour's skirmishing they completely discomfited the savages, with only the loss of one horse killed and two wounded.

The Indians are very chary of their lives; they usually gallop round and round the waggon, their bodies being bent down and sheltered behind their horses, to which they are always attached by stout leather thongs, so that if wounded they are carried off and do not fall into the enemy's hands. Their weapons are bows and arrows, and rifles, with which they are expert, but they prefer fighting at long range.

It is said that there are white men among them who

teach them to fight, and encourage them in their present rebellion, who have good telescopes, and signal by directing the rays of the sun from looking-glasses, reflecting from one to the other.

Riding for some miles every day, I had opportunities of conversing with the soldiers composing our escort.

ON THE LOOK-OUT.

They were generally from a volunteer regiment, and in every instance included two or three men of good education: probably all were able to read and write, and held decided views on public questions, which they discussed with intelligence.

The dress of our escort was at times little more than parti-coloured rags. At some places on the road between

Denver and Atchison, they did not start until half-an-hour after the stage had gone on; in one instance they were all drunk; on another occasion they were too lazy to bring their carbines, and would fire off their revolvers at marks on the road, leaving themselves quite defenceless.

One night we were awakened by a loud report close to our ears. We started up and seized our arms, but were quieted and soothed by the assurance that it was only a double-barrelled blunderbuss loaded with slugs which had gone off by accident, and blown out the side of the coach!

One day, as I rode on the right side of the sergeant in command of the escort, his revolver went off; the bullet pierced through the saddle, wounded his horse, and passed down close to my foot. For the remainder of that stage I rode on his left side.

Six days after starting, we rode through the pass in the Rocky Mountains called Bridger Pass. This is the watershed of North America.

Here we saw two tiny streams, within a few yards of each other: the one joins the Colorado, and flows into the Pacific; the other joins the Platte River and Mississippi, and flows into the Atlantic. This, then, was the summit of the Rocky Mountains.

Near this spot we came upon a covey of sage-hens; the whole detachment opened fire on them with rifles and revolvers, but they walked majestically away through the sage-brush unhurt.

The following day we reached Fort Halleck, where we

MANDAN INDIAN.

heard reports of Indians being in the neighbourhood; so our escort was increased.

After leaving this place, the barren aspect of the country somewhat changed; the hillsides were lightly timbered and picturesque, and the sage-brush was replaced by coarse prairie grass. There were many streams, so that the land appeared as if it might have been brought under cultivation by irrigation.

More or less gold is found in all these hills, which it will be profitable to mine when transport and provisions are cheaper. The reddish soil abounding in quartz is just like the gold-bearing earth of some parts of California. Coal is also found in the neighbourhood, and so near the surface that it is dug up and used as wanted at Fort Halleck.

On the ninth day we arrived at a romantic little station among some rocky hills, called Virginia Dale; after which we entered the prairie country.

These stations consist in most instances of only the stage-house and stables, and at the best there are but one or two houses besides. In themselves of no interest, they are nevertheless the only landmarks across a great continent, and may some day give their names to cities or districts. The houses are invariably loopholed between the logs; no man stirs out without at least a revolver, and everywhere one sees signs of being in a hostile land.

On the afternoon of the tenth day we reached Denver, a young and thriving town with many brick buildings.

It is built at a ford over the south fork of the Platte River.

Last year the water rose suddenly, carrying off some houses on its banks, and since then all new houses have been built on higher ground.

Denver is the centre of what is called the Pike's Peak mining district.

This formed a period in the long journey. Here was a fair inn, a daily newspaper, telegraphic communication, and iced drinks; but I was only two-thirds of the way across the uncivilised country, and was anxious to press on.

Early in the year there were Indian troubles between this and Atchison: the savages came in large bodies and drove off the stage-cattle, killed and horribly mutilated the station-keepers, and carried off the women. Lately, however, they have been comparatively peaceful. A Concord coach arrives and departs daily, and a small escort of only three or four men accompanies it.

After a day in Denver I left for Atchison.

Our journey was chiefly through rolling prairies, with but little variety—all sure to be brought under cultivation sooner or later. We saw several antelopes, and got a shot or two at them, but without damage to either party.

At Denver, we had heard by telegraph that a body of fifteen hundred Sioux Indians had attacked some troops at Platte Bridge, near Fort Laramer, about seventy miles from the stage-road, and defeated them with a loss of one officer and twenty-six privates killed, and sixteen

wounded. Along the road we found the telegraph operators and station-keepers in some alarm, fearing another Indian raid.

On the second day we reached Julesburg. Four days previously two waggons travelling near this place were attacked by a party of Sioux, the occupants were killed and shockingly mutilated, the waggons burned, and their contents carried off, with the team of horses.

On the fourth day we passed Fort Kearney, where is a small village. In the afternoon we stopped to dinner at a home-station, where we picked up another passenger, who travelled in the coach for a few miles. He studiously strove to pick a quarrel with me, which I as carefully avoided.

At last he abused me outright, saying I was not the sort of man for that country; that he knew quite well who I was; that there were too many of my sort in the country already; that he saw through my little game perfectly, &c.

I saw he had been drinking, so I laughed, and took no notice of him; and after he had got down I inquired of a fellow-passenger what I had done to provoke his wrath. He told me that I had mortally offended him by asking for a second plate off which to eat my tart, instead of using the same one I had for my meat, and that he believed me to be a New York travelling-clerk to a dry goods shop, and "putting on style" in the Far West.

On this overland journey I saw the roughest men I

ever saw in my life. I have been among gold miners and coal miners, and I have seen the lowest specimens of 'long-shore bargees, but I never met such utterly degraded and repulsive men as some of the stock-keepers on this road. Two or three generally live together; they are unmarried, and rarely see a woman. They never get hold of a book or a newspaper, unless it be one dropped by a passing traveller—whose baggage is not likely to contain much literature—and, as might be expected, they become thoroughly degraded and brutalised. I have always been able to make some headway with every class of people until I came across these men, and I must confess that, with the exception of the driver who brought us to grief in the river, I hardly met with a decent or civil word from any one of them.

In the evening we saw a body of about twenty horsemen a couple of miles distant, making for the road behind us. The driver walked his horses, in order that if they were Indians they might not think we were afraid of them, while we felt rather uncomfortable and got our arms ready. Presently, however, we opened out a hollow where was a military camp, so we concluded that the horsemen were either a cavalry picket or an Indian picket watching the soldiers.

An hour or two later we saw a body of thirty or forty Indians travelling northwards. They passed close to an emigrant train that we met, without attempting to molest them, probably deterred by the proximity of the soldiers.

After Fort Kearney we left the Platte, and followed

the course, first of the Little Blue and then of the Big Blue Rivers.

Our progress now was slow, as late rains had made the roads heavy, and swollen the streams so that some were impassable. The damp cherished the mosquitoes, which came about us in clouds, adding much to our discomfort. At night the bushes swarmed with fireflies, or, as Americans elegantly describe them, "lightning-bugs."

On the morning of the 6th we reached the banks of the Big Blue, and found upwards of twenty feet of water dashing down over the ford. A stout rope was stretched over it, and we went across one at a time, on a raft made of three shapeless logs nailed together, which our weight completely submerged. The swift current rushed by up to our knees, and of course some of our baggage got wet, but all crossed without accident.

Another coach was waiting for us, on the top of which we spread our wet things, and they dried quickly in the sun. On the following evening we drove into Atchison, and found ourselves once more in civilised parts.

A RIDE IN MEXICO.

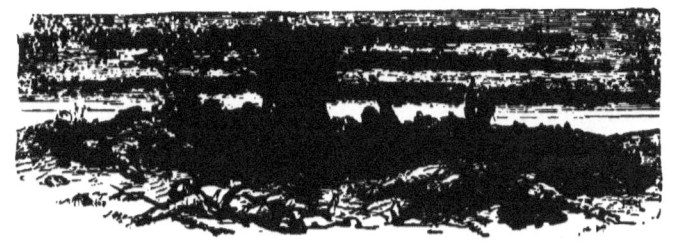

A RIDE IN MEXICO.

CHAPTER I.

AMONG ROBBERS AND REVOLUTIONS.

BY five A.M. we were ready, and our start was one of the prettiest scenes possible.

Pack-mules were kicking and twisting; saddle-horses held by armed servants; our party all armed with Henry rifles, carrying sixteen shots, and with revolvers; the crowd of lookers-on standing gaping round; Señor H. on his grey pony, with a huge umbrella strapped to the saddle; Ali, the Newfoundland dog, bustling about to see all was right; and the first crimson streaks of sunrise behind the old bell-tower.

Mrs. P. and I were both armed; it was a queer sensation buckling on a revolver for the first time; and notwithstanding the laughter that greeted my first appearance with a full-sized Smith and Wesson on my belt, I mean to stick to it; and am already beginning to look on it as my best friend.

For the first ten miles the order of march was this:—First, two armed men; then the five pack-mules, with their two drivers, also armed; then two of the gentlemen, Mrs. P. and I, in the same old phaeton that brought us from Manzanillo; the rest of our party, with Don Juan, another gentleman, and Mr. M., who is coming through to Guadalajara with us; and two more servants to bring up the rear.

At seven o'clock we changed horses for a pair which I am certain had never been driven before. To begin with, they would not start. Two of the servants then rode up, one on each side, and catching them by the heads, and flogging at the same time with the raw-hide whips they use here, got them off with a bounce at last.

Then they went for a little way full gallop, till our gentlemen were left far behind; when, coming to a slight rise, they stopped dead and began backing. Now, the harness being perfectly rotten and tied together with bits of string, the near horse slipped under the traces, turned completely round, and stared at us. Another grand effort, and they were started again at a furious pace; but in a minute Mrs. P. and I discovered that the near horse had not got the bit in his mouth at all, but had slipped it out, and it was hanging on his throat. Scream as we would to the *cochero*, he would not or could not understand us, but drove solemnly on, flogging the horses to a wilder pace, till at last, much to his astonishment, we dragged the reins from his hands, and as we fortunately were going up hill, the animals at last stopped.

A MEXICAN HUT.

The gentlemen then caught us up; the harness was "fixed up," and we set off once more, with Mr. Y. and Señor A. by our sides; but in about a mile the horses behaved so badly again that we could bear it no longer, and entreated to get on the mules. So we pulled up at a palm-thatched hut, where our steeds soon arrived.

Mine was a brown one, and very ugly, but a solemn and patient beast, who jogged along most comfortably if allowed to choose his own road. They paced about four miles an hour; and passing through fields of maize, frijoles, and sugar-cane, all irrigated and looking exquisitely green, we came at eleven A.M. to the La Quesaria, a large *hacienda* or plantation, 3,820 feet above the sea, seventeen miles from Colima.

This plantation employs 200 hands, and produces yearly 225 tons of clayed sugar, 78 tons of *panela* (coarse brown sugar), 50 tons of rice, and 1,200 barrels of rum.

We were not much reassured by the accounts of the road, which a priest told us was *muy peligroso* from robbers, and that the league and a half between La Quesaria and Tonila was the worst part of all. So, when we started, at one P.M., three servants were sent ahead as videttes; we all came next, with the baggage-mules, and the four other servants behind us—a party of fourteen in all.

In about a quarter of a mile we passed the Barranca (gorge) de la Quesaria, the first of any size we had yet come to; it was very steep, the road zigzagging down the side to the stream below. Then up the other side, and along a broad road between stone walls. Though a sharp look-out was kept, no robbers appeared.

Climbing up the further side, we rode into the little agricultural town of Tonila, and through its quaint streets of old houses, with crinkled Roman-tiled roofs and wooden corbels.

MEXICAN VEGETATION.

Out of Tonila we took a short cut across the slopes of the Volcano of Colima, which now towered up above us, with its two peaks of *fuego* and *nieve*, fire and snow. Smoke poured from a fissure low down on the side below the peak of "fire;" and near San Marcos the ground was quite grey with the dust which had fallen in clouds five weeks before, during the last eruption two months before. The country was open and bare of trees, except along the streams, which all cañon as they do in Colorado, the Spanish bayonet or yucca, growing to twenty feet, with many branches and fine heads of flowers.

Our only excitement during the march was just as we were turning up a hill, when two horsemen appeared at the top. They drew up. So did we, and the gentlemen all rode to the front. They hesitated, and seemed inclined to turn back; but finally reassured, every one declared, by my umbrella, which was unfurled in a most peaceable style, they came down the hill; and as they passed, with a pleasant though rather trembling *buenas tardes* (good evening), we saw it was only a poor fat old gentleman travelling with his servant, who had evidently been much more scared at us than we had been at them.

About 3.30 we caught the first sight of the hacienda of San Marcos, rising up white on a knoll of rock, over a mass of low buildings clustered together. What a view it was!

The volcano, with its two peaks and its pine-covered slopes, was on our left; and far down to the right, across rich sugar-fields, ran the dark line of the great Barranca de Beltran, with the mountains of Morelia rising rugged behind it. After half an hour more, over two small cañons and along an open plain, we jogged up to the hacienda, not at all sorry to ride in through the wide open, hospitable gates, and jump off under the orange-trees.

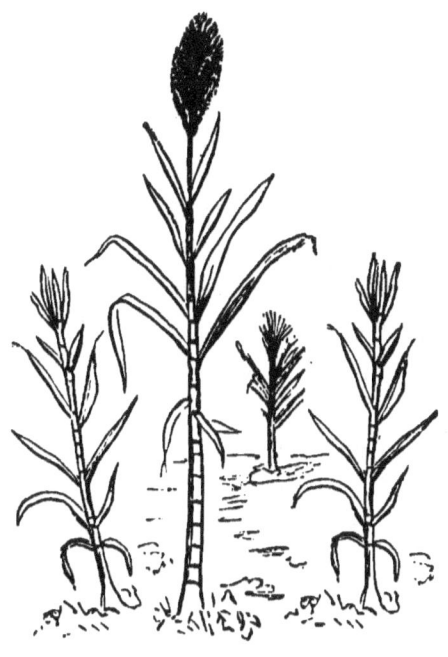

SUGAR CANES.

Don Mauricio G., the owner, was not in, but soon returned ; and his family being at Zapotlan, he placed the whole of his house " at our disposal."

San Marcos is a sugar plantation covering 22,000 acres, whose lands extend to the summit of the Volcano of

Colima. The slopes of the volcano are covered with pine. On the lands of San Marcos are 1,600 souls. The plantation employs 300 hands, and produces yearly 3,000 barrels of rum, 550,000 lbs. of sugar, besides corn and frijoles.

The hands employed in the sugar works are paid ten dollars (£2) per month, besides rations. Those working in the field earn five dollars per month and rations. These wages may be considered average prices for labour on the plantations in this region, of which San Marcos is a fair specimen.

On the 5th we had to get up at three A.M. for our start, but were amply repaid for the trouble by the picture which met our eyes as we came out into the piazza.

The whole court was lit up by two huge fires in iron cressets to light the men at the mill; for they were grinding cane all night; and the red glow and dancing shadows played upon the walls and towers of the Alto.

Close by, our servants were packing and saddling the mules and horses under the orange-trees. Our host, followed by a troop of dogs, was overseeing everything; servants ran about with cups of chocolate and plates of cakes; and some sleeper was still swinging in his hammock at the end of the piazza.

Severo, the "master of the horse," was a very fine-looking man—a Spaniard, six feet high, with blue eyes and light hair. His dress was a magenta shirt, with black in front; buckskin pantaloons, with rows of silver buttons and black embroidery down the leg; a short embroidered buckskin jacket; a rainbow-coloured scarf round his throat; a black belt, with silver-mounted pistol; and a sombrero, with silver embroidery. Altogether his was one of the most effective costumes I ever saw.

At four A.M. we set out to cross the famous *barrancas*, or gorges, as they would be called in England.

A road between fields of sugar-cane hedged with

ROAD IN A BARRANCA.

bananas, led us in half a mile to the brink of the Barranca of Tuxpan. It is about seven hundred feet deep, and the paved road is zigzagged down the almost perpendicular sides.

We preferred dismounting and walking, and even so could hardly keep our feet. At the stream which runs along the bottom we remounted.

At the top of the steep ascent of the Tuxpan we came on a long barren plateau of volcanic ash, and then descended into the great Barranca of Beltran, and kept some way along its "bench," a flat valley a mile wide, five hundred feet below the upper plateau, with the river in a yet deeper cleft on the right, and beyond it the impenetrable mountains of Michoacan, full of robbers and mountain lions.

The trees were full of parrots, and of the *chachalapa*, a handsome game-bird, as large as a cock pheasant, with a curious double larynx, which enables it to produce a hideous noise. Everywhere the alamanda was in blossom. Passing the little village of Platanar, with five hundred inhabitants, we turned down through a stream, then up to the high land again; and at Agosto entered the first pinery, at an elevation of three thousand five hundred to four thousand feet above sea-level.

A RIDE IN MEXICO.

CHAPTER II.

AMONG ROBBERS AND REVOLUTIONS.

SOON we came to the regular pine-barrens, and rode through them for some miles, passing two immense trains of mules. We met and passed during the day's journey a thousand animals, loaded with an average of three hundred pounds each, or a total of a hundred and fifty tons. These mule trains are continually robbed in passing the pine-barrens; and whenever we came to a sandy *arroyo*, or gulch, we kept a sharp look-out.

A band of robbers a week ago made this road almost impassable. They stopped every one who came along the road, and after robbing them, gagged them and bound them to the trees till night came; when they loosed one man, and, making off, left him to untie all his fellow-sufferers.

Wearied out with climbing up and down the barrancas, we were truly thankful to reach the last of them, the Barranca de Atenquique, at the bottom of which is a *paradero*, or a Mexican wayside inn.

Here the mules and horses were unladen, and trotted off to the stream, where they stamped about in the cool water to escape the flies. We meanwhile rested outside a miserable palm-thatched hut, as the house was too filthy to enter.

The mistress of the house, a great fat dirty woman, brought out some turkey stewed till it was almost black, in a sauce of red pepper so intensely hot that one feels as if one were positively eating fire. Some of our party, whose throats were hardened to Mexican cookery, thought this excellent; but we wretched ladies wept involuntary tears after a bit the size of a sixpence. In our luncheon basket we discovered one tin of sardines remained, and a few Albert biscuits. Then I plucked up courage, went into the filthy hut, and with Severo's help manufactured in an earthen pipkin some tea, which was very reviving; and thus we got our luncheon.

The pigs grunted round our feet; the chickens, whom their fat mistress called "Jews of Pollos," flew over our cups and plates; a large dog jumped in and out of the low doorway, and across our laps; and the picture of discomfort was completed when a horrible beggar-woman came and joined the group.

Arrived at the top of the barranca, four thousand feet above the sea, we found an old mud-waggon, with five mules, awaiting us; and, with a warning from the chief of our escort to have all arms in readiness, as the road was swarming with robbers, we set off for fifteen miles jolting into Zapotlan.

The road was indescribable; now through sandy tracks in the pineries, creeping along at three miles an hour, for we took five hours to do that wretched fifteen miles; then out of the forest and into a fresh misery, in the shape of a *pedrigal*, or stony place.

A pedrigal is a series of lava screes, where the hot lava has run over the country from some one of the innumerable volcanos which, active or extinct, appear all over Mexico. One of these was a wild tract, a mile or more wide, of horrible lava rocks, among low scrub of mimosa and nopal (prickly pear), yet in the very rocks themselves, where nothing else would grow, nestled the most exquisite cacti in endless variety.

Our escort previously had all agreed in assuring us that the pedrigal was the most likely place on the whole road for the robbers to attack us, so that our feelings were not exactly comfortable when we discovered that they and our mules had gone round by another road a quarter of a mile off, and just in this place our wretched old coach broke down utterly. The cochero got down; the muchacho got down; we all got out; everybody suggested something different; and I retired to a convenient rock near by with one of the rifles, and tried to imagine what I should do if the robbers pounced upon us.

At last the escort came up, their mouths full of some sweet fruit, something like a yellow plum, which they found on a tree near by; and, after gallantly presenting us with some of their spoils, the united energies of the whole party succeeded in patching up the stage, and on we went again.

A PEDRIGAL.

At last we arrived at Zapotlan, where, later in the evening, came startling news.

The day after we left Colima it was attacked by the Pronunciados under Julio Garcia. They expect that he may arrive here to-morrow afternoon or evening.

Next morning, scouting parties were out all round the

town, and the troops were under arms; but the troops could not do much good in case of an attack, for their rule is to retreat to the barracks under such circumstances, and shutting themselves up securely, to leave the town in the hands of the revolutionists.

A PEDRIGAL.

Yet, strange to say, nobody seems to mind much. There was no excitement, and things went on much as usual. The women sat on the pavement selling fruit and flowers. The men lounged about gossiping over the fountain, or drinking *pulque*. The very soldiers loiter at *posada* doors. And all this, with an enemy advancing from two sides: not to kill them, it is true, but to levy a heavy sum on their city, and take what they will.

All we could do was to wait quietly for the stage, in which we were to start the following day at one A.M., and under advice we hid all our arms for fear of the Pronunciados, till we should get to Zacoalco, where the danger of meeting them ceases, and the real danger from the "ladrones" (robbers) begins. The former, every

PRONUNCIADOS ATTACKING A TRAVELLER.

one says, will not annoy us at all if we meet them, but would of course take our arms if they could get them, and search for Government mails or property. But the robbers between Sta. Ana Acatlan and Guadalajara are a very different matter.

The stage is robbed by them nearly every day. Yesterday it came through safe; but the day before it was attacked by fourteen robbers, and the seven passengers were robbed of all they had. They did not make any resistance, and had no escort; but we shall have an escort, and, if attacked, shall certainly make a resistance.

Zapotlan is a thriving place, of twenty-five thousand inhabitants, standing at a height of nearly five thousand feet, on the slope of some hills overlooking a magnificently rich plain, on the further side of which, to the east of south, rises the Volcano of Colima.

IN THE ZAPOTLAN MARKET.

There are some very good shops, and a pretty market, with heaps of peppers, tomatoes, limes, zapotes, etc., on the ground, shaded by a square of *tule* matting on a stick, something like a Chinese umbrella. This matting is made from the *tule* reed, which grows in all the fresh-water lagoons, and is plaited by the Indians into mats, which are called *petates*, and also into *tompiates*, baskets the shape of a bucket, and of every size from that of a teacup to a bushel.

On the second night by two A.M., with no feeling of regret, we bade farewell to Zapotlan, and started in a regular American Concord stage-coach. We were a party of nine. Our only other fellow-passenger was an old Señora, who sat in a corner by me, and puffed cigarettes all the day long.

For the first part of the road we kept our arms out. There was no light for a couple of hours, except from the stars: but we could not sleep; every nerve seemed strained to catch some sight or sound which might denote robbers. Where we stopped to change mules especially, we were on the look-out, as the ladrones are very fond of making a rush upon the coach as it stands still.

A regular plan was arranged in case of an attack. We were all to fire at once, without giving them time to come near. "Fire low and keep cool" were the orders. Then we ladies, if the ruffians did not run at once, were to throw ourselves on the floor, and fire from under cover, while the gentlemen got out to fight.

Our road led us up and over a steep divide, some miles from Zapotlan; and just before dawn, as we were going down the further side, between high cactus hedges, we had a "scare;" for in the grey light we saw a man drop suddenly into the ditch behind us. He was evidently on the look-out for us, but not liking the muzzles of the rifles out of the windows, let us go by untouched.

At sunrise we reached Seyula, a pretty old town, and

changed mules. Here the news was worse and worse. The Government troops were marching south on the town; beyond them the Pronunciados were in force on the road; and beyond them again the country was swarming with robbers in bands of any number from two to two hundred.

Leaving Seyula, all the arms were hidden, in hopes of saving them should the Pronunciados catch us. The rifles were wrapped in a *serape*, and stowed under the back seat; but we kept our pistols on us, concealing them under our clothes.

A little way from the town we came up to the Lago de Seyula, a salt lake, with soda flats all round. A few miles along the lake we met the Government troops, a fine body of cavalry, and their colonel confirmed the reports of the road we had heard.

The alkali dust was perfectly choking, scorching the very skin; and we muffled our faces in handkerchiefs, and so jolted on hour after hour over rocks and gulleys, and in one place through half a mile of heaps of broken pottery, layer upon layer, several feet thick, imbedded in loose sandy soil, till, at eleven A.M., we drove into the village of Cebollas (onions).

We pulled up in front of a poor-looking house, with a young fellow lolling on the window-seat, where breakfast was preparing, of which we were in need. We dragged our stiffened limbs into the house, where we sat down to a most uninviting meal of omelet and dried beef.

Just as we did so, however, we heard a clatter in the

courtyard, and in rode two Pronunciados and dismounted. In a minute, two more and an officer appeared in front of the windows; and they then sent in word they wished " our permission" to search the coach for arms.

Those of the gentlemen who were not out already went out instantly. Every possible argument was used; but Chavarin, the major, said he had orders to come and take the rifles. Expostulation was in vain, resistance out of the question; for, though we could easily have overpowered this party, they were but the outpost of another body. So the five rifles and two pistols were soon handed in through the window, to be taken by the women who were serving us, and stowed away in an' inner room.

It was evidently a pre-arranged thing, and the whole pack were in league; the women were so very reassuring to us in the way they hovered about us while all this was going on, begging the "Señoritas to fear nothing, there was no danger;" and the young man in the window, who watched us so closely, and then disappeared, I cannot help fancying was in the secret also. In fact, we found out afterwards that our party and their precious repeating rifles had been watched and followed all the way from the coast.

Major Chavarin was dressed in a linen jacket, and high embroidered boots over linen pantaloons; was well armed; and on his left wrist wore a suggestive bracelet —a leather strip about an inch wide, ornamented with a hundred or more copper caps. His men were a despicable

MIRAGE ON THE ALKALI PLAINS.

set of ruffians, in any kind of dress over military trousers, wretchedly armed with old muzzle-loading carbines, and they were all drunk.

Chavarin promised, however, to escort us towards Zacoalco, through the worst bit of robber country, and half promised that he would there give back two of the rifles. So on we drove in blazing sun over the alkali plains, by the side of a lake in which we watched the reflections of trees in its bright water, and the ripples on its shore.

Suddenly some one said—

"Why, there are clouds of dust blowing across the lake!"

And as he spoke the water began to fade away. Suddenly the view changed into a horrible waste of soda sand. Our rippling lake had been only a mirage.

As we were looking out at this strange sight, up rode three of the Pronunciados, and said that the major had been obliged to turn back, and that they must go too, being alarmed at a cloud of dust ahead, which they thought must be Government troops, and demanded our ammunition.

That, of course, was refused; and fearing our revolvers, they sneaked off, leaving us comparatively defenceless at the very edge of the robber-infested country. There was nothing for it but to get on as fast as possible. Each man had a pistol, thirty-six shots in all; and I kept the ammunition in my lap, to be ready to load again if need be.

We now turned into a road between stone walls and

bushes, on to the bare hillside from which all trees had been burnt or cut to leave no shelter. We strained our eyes at each gap, expecting to be pounced upon!

We soon stopped for a *remuda* at a village of three or four huts, and then saw a suspicious white rag on the hill. The people said, "Oh, it was only clothes washing;" but one of our party went up and found it was tied on to a rail stuck upright—a rather curious way of washing clothes.

When the journey was resumed we were made to barricade ourselves with cushions and valises, with orders if firing began, to throw ourselves flat down and heap the blankets over us. The gentlemen got out and went ahead in a skirmish line up the hill for a mile or so; but nothing befell us.

Here the poor *cochero* entreated them to go inside, for he said, "If we are attacked, and you fire, and make me drive on instead of stopping, as Mexicans always do, to allow the coach to be robbed, then the robbers will certainly shoot me as I come back to-morrow."

It was with no slight feeling of relief that in about two hours more we entered the town of Sta. Ana Acatlan and mingled in its street and market crowded with people. At the diligence office we halted, and—thanks to our letters of introduction to the chief man of the town—we were provided with an excellent escort.

In an hour twenty-eight trusty men mounted on little, tough, spirited horses, well armed with musket, pistol, and *machete* (a strong short sword), and under the command of an old army officer, were assembled in the street ready to take us to Guadalajara.

When all was ready we clattered off through the streets and up a hill towards the Coronilla Mountain.

At every turn we met ox and mule trains, who had all been robbed that day, the drivers giving different accounts of the number of the ladrones, and looking at us with pity. But our good escort kept up gallantly, forming front and

ATTACK ON TRAVELLER BY ROBBERS.

rearguard in the bad places, and dodging along to cut off corners in the safe ones; and so we crossed the Divide under the Coronilla in safety.

Down in the valley below we were told to be on the look-out; a robbery had been committed in the morning, and the ground was strewn with papers left from the plunder.

Our escort formed in single file on either side of us,

and some skirmished along behind a high cactus hedge, till we came to a robber town, Santa Cruz.

Santa Cruz is a miserable place, with adobe houses, for the most part roofless, looking quite worthy of their owners' trade. On the top of the church we saw four men evidently watching us, and outside the town two or

NIGHT AMONG THE PINERIES.

three more on horseback sneaking off into the distance, thinking us too strong to be meddled with.

An hour after sunset we stopped to change horses at Santa Augustin, another robber den, thankful for even a few minutes' rest from the jolting of the coach.

Here, whilst we got a cup of chocolate, our escort halted close round us to prevent a rush on the coach. Armed men were hanging about the doors of the houses, looking at us with longing eyes.

With six stout ponies, on we went again, getting snatches of sleep between the bits of pedrigal.

I think I had been dozing some quarter of an hour when we stopped, and up rode the Captain to put us on the watch, as we were coming to a bad barranca. I rubbed my sleepy eyes open and looked out. It was a wild scene. We were tearing on with our half-broken ponies over an open road; our escort, with carbines unslung and ready to fire in a moment, galloped alongside, with serapes over their shoulders to keep off the cold air, and most of them masked with handkerchiefs to keep off the dust.

This place we passed in safety, and dozed off again from time to time, till, on coming to the city outposts, six miles from Guadalajara, we were stopped, and a "passport of arms" demanded by the picket. This we had not got; but when it was explained who and what we were, the sergeant in command let us go by, as one of the worst places was still to come, and to have passed it without arms would have been mere folly. Nothing, however, occurred.

At ten P.M. we rattled down the streets of the capital of Jalisco, our muchacho on the box carrying a flaming torch, which left a trail of sparks behind him, and our faithful escort keeping close around us.

THE END.